CARBON CAPTURE, UTILIZATION, AND STORAGE GAME CHANGERS IN ASIA

2020 COMPENDIUM OF TECHNOLOGIES AND ENABLERS

ASIAN DEVELOPMENT BANK

ADB

Contents

Figures and Boxes

Foreword

The Asian Development Bank (ADB) supports low-carbon development alternatives for Asia and the Pacific. Carbon capture, utilization, and storage (CCUS) was identified as an important emerging technology for low-carbon growth in Asia. ADB has supported its promotion in Asia through a dedicated Carbon Capture and Storage Fund (CCS Fund). The fund is supported through contributions from the Department for Business, Energy and Industrial Strategy, Government of the United Kingdom.

Since the inception of the CCS Fund, ADB has supported Bangladesh, the People's Republic of China, India, Indonesia, Mongolia, Pakistan, Thailand, and Viet Nam in exploring CCUS opportunities through knowledge sharing, capacity building events, CCUS-related publications, and support to pilot projects. As a result, it has become clear that CCUS is a continually evolving technology that developing member countries (DMCs) should be made aware of.

Carbon Capture, Utilization, and Storage Game Changers in Asia: 2020 Compendium of Technologies and Enablers showcases new and innovative low-carbon technologies that are being demonstrated or are in the early commercialization stage. The collection features key highlights, advantages, applications, the status of development and commercialization, and potential for deployment in Asia.

The compendium aims to promote technology investment, transformation, and deployment, and identify support needed to bring the technologies to the pilot and/or early commercialization stages. This report introduces the latest technologies to policymakers and practitioners to assist in the deployment of this emerging low-carbon technology at a national level.

Yongping Zhai
Chief of Energy Sector Group
Sustainable Development and Climate Change Department
Asian Development Bank

Acknowledgments

This publication titled *Carbon Capture, Utilization, and Storage Game Changers in Asia: 2020 Compendium of Technologies and Enablers* was prepared by the consultant team from the Asian Development Bank (ADB) under regional Technical Assistance 9686: Integrated High Impact Innovation in Sustainable Energy Technology (Subproject 2): Prefeasibility Analysis for Carbon Capture, Utilization, and Storage supported by the Department of Business, Energy and Industrial Strategy, Government of the United Kingdom, through the Carbon Capture and Storage Fund under the Clean Energy Financing Partnership Facility.

The main contributors to this compendium are 8 Rivers (Adam Goff); CarbonCure Technologies (Kaja Salovsky); Carbon Infinity (David Isikowitz); Compact Carbon Capture AS (Kari Forthun, Torleif Madsen); École Polytechnique Fédérale de Lausanne (Francois Marèchal, Shivom Sharma); Econic Technologies Limited (Rowena Sellens, Leigh S. Taylor); LanzaTech (Sangeet Jain, Prabhakar Nair); Liquid Wind AB (Tuya Bold, Allie Downes); OGCI (Julien Perez, Delia Meth-Cohn, Jason dela Cruz); Osaki CoolGen Corporation (Haruhito Kubota, Takehisa Okino); and Shell Global Solutions International B.V. (Stacy Barnes).

Guidance and support in the preparation of this compendium were provided by Woochong Um, Director General concurrently Chief Compliance Officer (ADB); Robert Guild, Chief Sector Officer (ADB); Yongping Zhai, Chief of Energy Sector Group (ADB); Andrew Jeffries, Country Director (ADB); Sujata Gupta, Director (ADB); Kee-Yung Nam, Principal Energy Specialist (ADB); Xuedu Lu, Lead Climate Change Specialist (ADB); Jinmiao Xu, Energy Specialist (ADB); Charity Torregosa, Senior Energy Officer (ADB); Amparo Dato, Senior Operations Coordination Officer (ADB); Maria Dona Aliboso, Operations Analyst (ADB); Angelica Apilado, Senior Operations Assistant (ADB); Darshak Mehta, Consultant (ADB); Remife De Guzman, Consultant (ADB); and, Dan Brian Millison, Consultant (ADB).

Publication of this compendium was guided and supported by Duncan McLeod, Communications Specialist (ADB); Cynthia Hidalgo, Senior Communications Officer (ADB); Noren Jose, Associate Communications Officer (ADB); Anthony Victoria, Communications Coordinator (ADB); Rodel Bautista, Senior Communications Assistant (ADB); Ma. Katrina Fernando, Communications Assistant (ADB); and Oliver Xavier Reyes, Consultant (ADB). Editing and layout were supported by Melanie Kelleher, copyeditor; Joel Pinaroc, proofreader; Lumina Datamatics, typesetter; and Michael Cortes, cover designer.

Abbreviations

CAPEX	capital expenditure
CCS	carbon capture and storage
CCUS	carbon capture, utilization, and storage
CO	carbon monoxide
CO_2	carbon dioxide
DAC	direct air capture
H_2	hydrogen
IGCC	integrated coal gasification combined cycle
IGFC	integrated gasification and combined cycle and fuel cell
$mtCO_2$	million tons of carbon dioxide
MW	megawatt
LHV	lower heating value
t	ton*
SOFC	solid oxide fuel cell

*Note: "ton" refers to "metric ton" equivalent to 1,000 kilograms.

Overview

This compendium deals with four interesting carbon dioxide capture technologies, five carbon dioxide utilization technologies, one utilization storage technology, and one enabler concept. The technologies presented are in various stages, ranging from research and development to commercial deployment. The enabler concept introduced in this compendium is an initiative to accelerate collaboration and deployment of CCUS. The technologies and enablers included in this compendium were furnished by CCUS technology providers and enablers through their responses to an e-mail questionnaire prepared by the consultant team of the Asian Development Bank (ADB) through regional technical assistance (TA 9686-REG), Integrated High Impact Innovation in Sustainable Energy Technology (Subproject 2): Prefeasibility Analysis for Carbon Capture, Utilization, and Storage.

ADB would like to clarify that the compendium is not exhaustive. Other ideas are available and may also be added to this but—because of time constraints— they are not added here. ADB looks forward to other opportunities to add to this collection of ideas on CCUS, which could help ADB developing member countries achieve low-carbon growth.

Game-Changing Carbon Dioxide Capture Technologies

Solid Sorbent Technology for Postcombustion Carbon Dioxide Capture

Technology provider

Shell Global Solutions with ViennaGreenCO$_2$ Consortium Members

Technology description

The solid sorbent technology is an innovative process that separates carbon dioxide (CO_2) from flue gas streams in a continuous temperature swing adsorption fluidized bed process using a solid adsorbent, and delivers high capture performance, lower capture costs, and low emissions. At low temperatures (about 50°C), CO_2 is first adsorbed in a first multistaged fluidized bed (adsorber) where heat is released due to the exothermicity of the adsorption reaction. The adsorbent is then transported in a riser to a second multistaged fluidized bed (desorber) via heat exchangers, where the previously bound CO_2 is released using steam at a temperature of 120°C. In this way, the adsorbent is regenerated (in a continuous process) and can be returned to the adsorber where it is again available for CO_2 capture. A fluidizable solid sorbent material is used where CO_2 can be very selectively bound to active amine groups that are tethered on the sorbent surface. The sorbent used displays high temperature and mechanical stability and as a result, produces very low emissions without the need for expensive post-treatment. The process contains no liquid water; therefore, lower-cost construction materials can be used compared to liquid amine technologies.

Technology highlights and advantages

It was demonstrated that the new process can separate over 90% of the CO_2 from the industrial gas and that this CO_2 has a purity of over 95% (dry basis), even at inflow concentrations of less than 4% by volume. Without any flue gas post-treatment, the atmospheric emissions from this process were significantly less than 1 milligram/normal cubic meter (mg/Nm^3) of ammonia and below the detection limit (< 0.2 mg/Nm^3) for other potential degradation products. The CO_2 was found to be—in principle—suitable for greenhouse fertilization.

Box 1: Shell Global Solutions Solid Sorbent Technology for Postcombustion Carbon Dioxide Capture Key Features

Technology Highlights

- Separates over 90% of CO_2 from industrial gases
- Achieves over 95% CO_2 purity
- Costs 25% lower than liquid amine separation technologies

Development Stage

- Commercial demonstration

Sectors of Application

- Postcombustion flue gas applications

Figure 1: Solid Sorbent Carbon Dioxide Capture Schematic Diagram

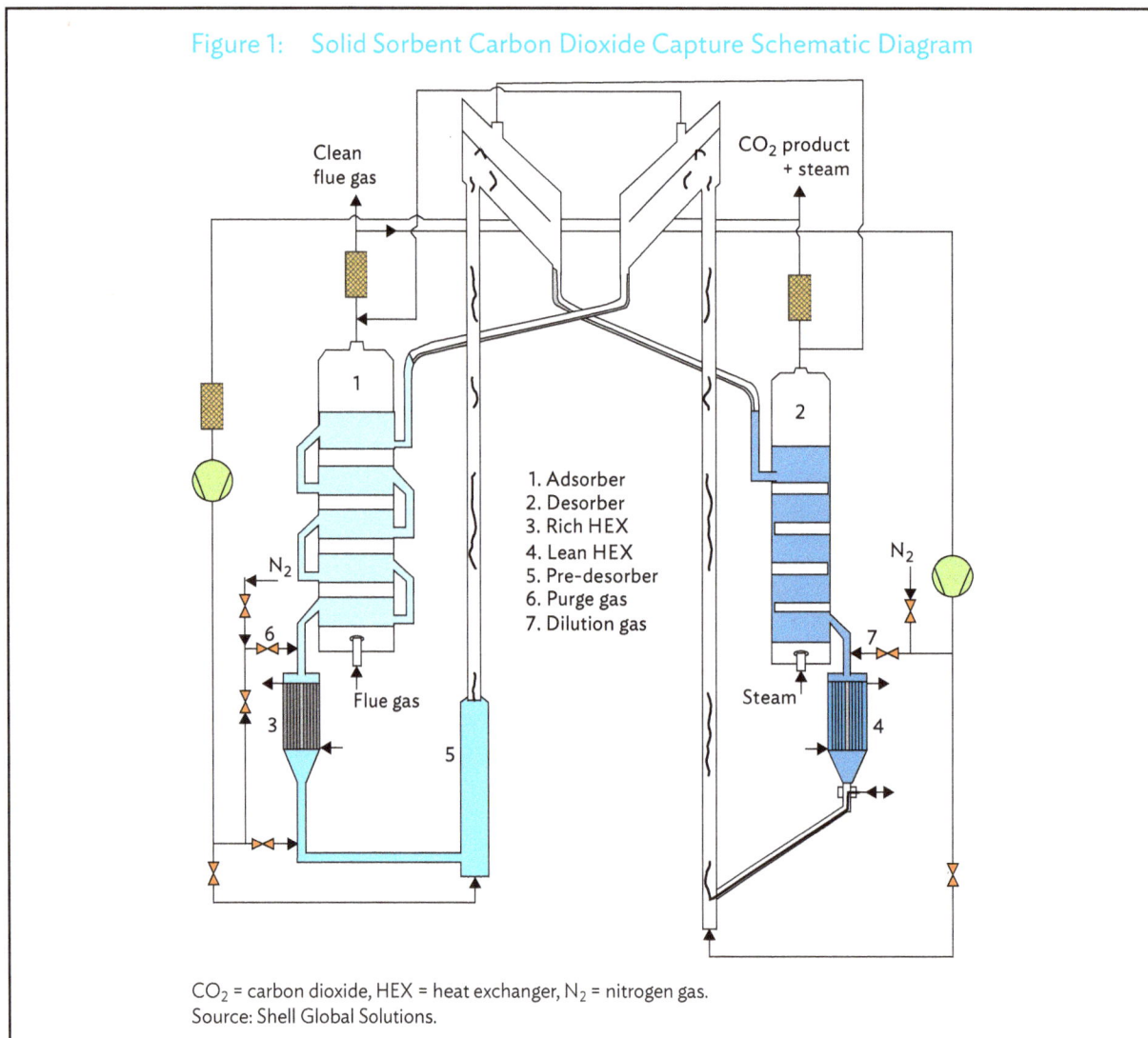

Clean
flue gas

CO$_2$ product
+ steam

1
2

1. Adsorber
2. Desorber
3. Rich HEX
4. Lean HEX
5. Pre-desorber
6. Purge gas
7. Dilution gas

N$_2$
N$_2$

6
7

3
4

Flue gas
5
Steam

CO$_2$ = carbon dioxide, HEX = heat exchanger, N$_2$ = nitrogen gas.
Source: Shell Global Solutions.

Related costs

Economic assessment of the technology has shown that separation costs per ton of CO$_2$ are up to 25% lower compared to state-of-the-art liquid amine technologies.

Potential application in Asia and the world

The technology applies to all postcombustion flue gas sources.

Status and next steps

Now that the ViennaGreenCO$_2$ project has been completed, the pilot plant will be transferred to the Netherlands and recommissioned to capture CO$_2$ from another industrial site. In parallel, Shell will continue to work in partnerships to further mature this technology and is planning to develop a demonstration project at a significantly larger scale (about 150 tons/day CO$_2$ capture). The TulipGreenCO$_2$ demonstration project will be the final upscaling step before deployment of the technology at full commercial scale.

Challenges in scale-up and deployment

The solid sorbent technology has shown potential for delivering high performance with lower costs and low emissions. Further de-risking will be done on larger scale cold flow models of the fluidized bed reactors to ensure good gas and solid distribution as well as efficient heat transfer. Shell's ambition is to be a net-zero carbon company by 2050. In support of this ambition—and continuing the collaborative approach—the TulipGreenCO$_2$ project will provide an opportunity for parties with similar ambitions to partner in the development of game-changing CO$_2$ capture technology. Engaging with potential partners across the CCUS value chain will be a focus of the project.

Technology provider background

The now completed ViennaGreenCO$_2$ consortium project aimed at designing, constructing, operating a circa 1 ton/day pilot CO$_2$ capture plant, and evaluating the suitability of produced CO$_2$ for greenhouse fertilization in Austria. After promising lab experiments in 2013, the consortium project launched in 2015. The team consisted of two universities (Vienna University of Technology-TU Wien, and the University of Natural Resources and Life Sciences-BOKU), a technology provider (Shell Global Solutions International), a plant manufacturer (Bertsch Energy), a heat integration specialist (M-tec), an end-user (Wien Energie), and potential CO$_2$ off-takers (LK projekt and LGV Frischgemuese).

Contact person:
Stacy Barnes
Commercial Lead Breakthrough CO$_2$ Capture Technology
E-mail: Stacy.Barnes2@Shell.com

Suggestions for further reading

- Shell. 2020. *Positive results from the ViennaGreenCO$_2$ pilot plant.* YouTube. 2 June. https://www.youtube.com/watch?v=tv6mEAsCP5U.
- Energy Innovation Austria. 2017. ViennaGreenCO$_2$. *New separation process to capture carbon dioxide from exhaust gases.* https://www.energy-innovation-austria.at/article/viennagreenco$_2$-2/?lang=en.
- Shell. 2018. *The "ViennaGreenCO$_2$" Pilot Plant for Separating Carbon Dioxide Goes into Operation in Simmering* (translated to English). 21 June. https://www.shell.at/medien/shell-presseinformationen/2018/vienna-green-co$_2$-pilotanlage-eroffnung.html.
- The Oil and Gas Climate Initiative. 2020. https://www.linkedin.com/posts/the-oil-and-gas-climate-initiative_positive-results-from-viennagreenco$_2$-pilot-activity-6684437763212775424-Af5y/.
- A. Bhalodi and K. Grigoriadou and M. Infantino and J. van de Graaf and S. Van Paasen. 2018. 14th International Conference on Greenhouse Gas Control Technologies, GHGT-14 paper: *Process development for large scale solid sorbent post combustion CO$_2$ capture technology for application to natural gas fired power stations.* https://papers.ssrn.com/sol3/papers.cfm?abstract_id=3366391.

Carbon Dioxide Capture from Internal Combustion Engine Exhaust

Technology provider
École Polytechnique Fédérale de Lausanne, Switzerland

Technology description
The proposed carbon dioxide (CO_2) capture system can capture 90% CO_2 from internal combustion engines without any energy penalty. An internal combustion engine has a typical efficiency of about 30%, which means 70% of fuel energy is lost as waste heat (exhaust gases and cooling system). The system includes a temperature swing adsorption (TSA) cycle, heat recovery from exhaust gases, Rankine cycle, heat pump, and product CO_2 compression. Amine-doped adsorbents are used for CO_2 capture, as they show good performance in the presence of water. As shown in Figure 2, the Rankine cycle uses waste heat from exhaust gases and produces mechanical power. Part of the mechanical power generated by the Rankine cycle is used to produce cold utility using a CO_2-based heat pump. This cold utility is used to remove the heat of adsorption and cool the exhaust stream to condense the water. The remaining mechanical power generated by the Rankine cycle is used to compress and liquefy the product CO_2.

TSA is an emerging technology for CO_2 capture that requires low-grade waste heat that may be available close to the CO_2 emission source (such as heat from exhaust gases). In a TSA cycle, cold exhaust gases are passed through the adsorbent bed, where CO_2 is adsorbed in the material and the remaining gases are released into the environment. Once the adsorbent bed is saturated with CO_2, it is heated to recover the CO_2 from the material. After CO_2 recovery from the adsorbent bed, it is cooled down from the desorption temperature to the adsorption temperature. Note that heat is removed (at low temperature) during the adsorption step, whereas heat is supplied (at high temperature) during the desorption step of the TSA cycle.

Box 2: Ecole Polytechnique Federale de Lausanne Carbon Dioxide Capture Key Features

Technology Highlights
- Energy self-sufficient, requires no external power
- Can be integrated into mobility systems
- Captured CO_2 can be transformed into liquid or gaseous fuel

CO_2 Capture
- Up to 90% of emitted CO_2

Development Stage
- Research and development

Sectors of Application
- Transportation
- Shipping
- Power
- Industries

A CO_2 capture system with liquid storage can be integrated into different types of vehicles such as cars, trucks, buses, ships, and trains. The added weight of the capture system with liquid storage includes the weights of CO_2, the storage tank, and adsorbent material. The system may also be used for CO_2 capture from other sources, such as ships, refineries, power plants, and cement and aluminum industries.

Technology highlights and advantages

(i)   Up to 90% of the produced CO_2 can be captured.
(ii)   The system has energy self-sufficiency and does not require any external power.
(iii) The exergy analysis shows that there is an opportunity by system integration to generate cold, heat, and work that is needed to capture CO_2 using the energy available in the exhaust gases.

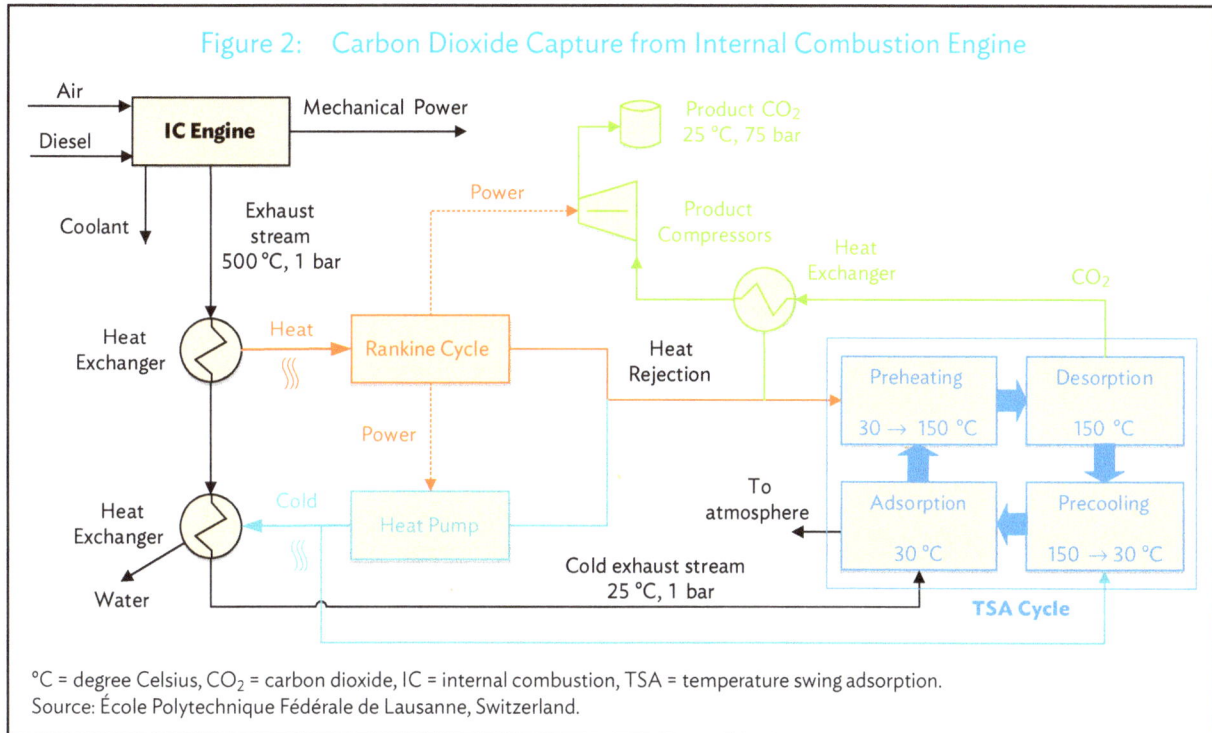

Figure 2:   Carbon Dioxide Capture from Internal Combustion Engine

°C = degree Celsius, CO$_2$ = carbon dioxide, IC = internal combustion, TSA = temperature swing adsorption.
Source: École Polytechnique Fédérale de Lausanne, Switzerland.

(iv)   The system can be integrated into the overall mobility system (fuel to internal combustion engine to CO$_2$ capture to CO$_2$ conversion to fuel), where captured CO$_2$ can be recycled as liquid or gaseous fuel produced using excess renewable energy.

(v)   The CO$_2$ capture system can be a retrofit option for internal combustion engines of trucks, buses, and ships without any major changes in the existing vehicles.

Process diagram

The concept of the CO$_2$ capture system shown in Figure 2 includes exhaust cooling, Rankine cycle, heat pump, TSA cycle, and product CO$_2$ compression. Components of these systems include turbines, compressors, heat exchangers, vessels, and adsorbent materials. Details of the CO$_2$ capture system can be found in Sharma and Maréchal (Frontiers in Energy Research 7:143, 2019).

Related costs

The proposed system can be a cost-effective solution, without requiring major changes to existing vehicles. The CO$_2$ capture system has turbines, compressors,

heat exchangers, vessels, and adsorbent material. Different industries have mastered the cost-effective and mass production of turbines, compressors, heat exchangers, and vessels. These parts of the system might be available commercially or can be produced in the required sizes.

Potential application in Asia and other regions

(i)   This solution can be used in trucks, buses, trains, and ships, and can be an interim solution before the commercial emergence of alternative technologies such as hydrogen and fuel cells.

(ii)   The product CO$_2$ from the system can be sequestered underground or used as feedstock to produce gas or liquid green fuels and chemicals. CO$_2$ can be converted into different carbon-based fuels using renewable electricity.

Status and next steps

The research group of François Maréchal at École Polytechnique Fédérale de Lausanne is in the process of creating a start-up company that will focus on prototype and commercial development of the CO_2 capture technology.

Challenges in scale-up and deployment

The main obstacle is the adsorbent material cost. Currently, there is no mass production of adsorbent materials. These adsorbent materials are produced for laboratory experiments, but their mass production could be cheaper as high purity is not needed for real-life applications.

Technology provider background

François Maréchal heads a team of 25 researchers of process and energy systems engineering at École Polytechnique Fédérale de Lausanne. F. Maréchal has published about 320 scientific papers (H-index 42). Research activities are focused on the development of computer-aided process and energy systems design methods, by applying process integration and optimization techniques.

Contact Person/s:
François Maréchal (francois.marechal@epfl.ch)
Shivom Sharma (shivomsharma.iitr@gmail.com)

Suggestions for further reading

- S. Sharma and F. Maréchal. 2019. *Carbon Dioxide Capture from Internal Combustion Engine Exhaust Using Temperature Swing Adsorption.* Front. Energy Res. 7:143. doi:10.3389/fenrg.2019.00143. [Open Access].
- S. Sharma and F. Maréchal. 2018. *System for CO_2 capture from internal combustion engine.* Submitted as European Patent (Application no 18203243.3 – 1104, application date 30.10.2018).
- L. Wang, Y. Zhang, M. Pérez-Fortes, P. Aubin, T.E. Lin, Y. Yang, F. Maréchal, and Y. Van herle. 2020. *Reversible solid-oxide cell stack based power-to-x-to-power systems: Comparison of thermodynamic performance.* Applied Energy 275.

Compact and Modular Scalable Carbon Dioxide Capture Technology

Technology provider
Compact Carbon Capture AS—A Baker Hughes Venture (CCC)

Technology description
Compact Carbon Capture has transformed the process equipment used in post-combustion carbon capture by introducing rotation and high G-forces to capture CO_2. The G-forces are created in several cross-flow rotating packed beds. Solvent is introduced from the center and flung outwards toward the perimeter in a horizontal direction. The flue gas moves vertically from the bottom to the top (Figure 3). The high G-forces allow for the application of highly viscous solvents that improve the process efficiency. Higher solvent concentration results in faster absorption rates. When this is combined with the compactness introduced by the process intensification, a considerably lower solvent volume is needed, and the pump capacity needed for solvent transfer is reduced.

The compact stripper is a combined reboiler and desorber unit that can operate at higher pressures and handle high viscosity solvents (Figure 4). High-speed rotation of the stripper unit introduces high G-forces to the solvent regeneration, and the retention time of the solvent is less than 10 seconds. Operating at higher pressure, the stripped CO_2 can be delivered at a pressure of up to 5 bar(g),[1] saving energy in the compression and liquefaction steps. The product is a high purity (>99%) CO_2 stream.

Technology highlights and advantages
The High-G technology of 3C increases capture efficiency, allowing for up to 90% reduction in the size of the absorption and desorption columns.

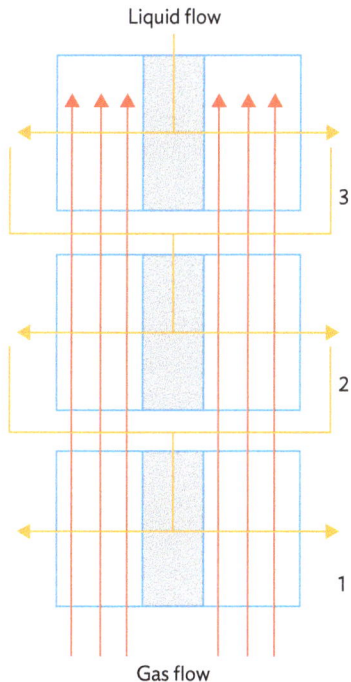

Figure 3:   Cross-Flow Absorber Process

Liquid flow

3

2

1

Gas flow

Note: The red lines indicate gas flows in a vertical direction. The yellow lines indicate solvent flows through all stages from top to bottom in a horizontal direction. The cross-flow absorber process (CFA) uses several stages to emulate a counter-flow process.
Source: Compact Carbon Capture AS—A Baker Hughes Venture.

Box 3: Compact Carbon Capture Key Features

Technology Highlights
- Compact
- Up to 75% smaller than conventional amine capture technologies
- Up to 50% CAPEX reduction

Development Stage
- Pilot demonstration

Sectors of Application
- Energy
- CO_2-emitting industries
- Shipping

---

[1]   Bar(g) refers to gauge pressure measured in bar. Gauge pressure is the pressure measured relative to atmospheric pressure.

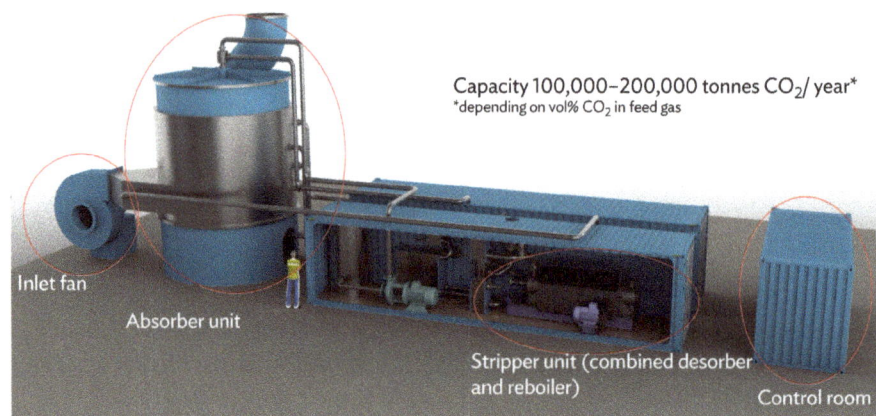

Figure 4:   Rendering of Compact Carbon Capture Plant at Industrial Scale

Capacity 100,000–200,000 tonnes CO_2/ year*
*depending on vol% CO_2 in feed gas

Inlet fan

Absorber unit

Stripper unit (combined desorber and reboiler)

Control room

CO_2 = carbon dioxide, vol% = percent by volume.
Source: Compact Carbon Capture AS—A Baker Hughes Venture.

Major advantages and key features of the CCC technology (compared to conventional technology):

(i)   90% +/- 10% CO_2 capture rate (depending on CO_2 concentration in flue gas).
(ii)   Up to 75% reduction in the overall size of the capture plant compared to conventional amine technology.
(iii) Up to 50% reduction in capital expenditure (CAPEX).
(iv)   The possibility to reduce operating expenses significantly by using new, viscous, and efficient solvents.
(v)   Reduced lead time through standardized and containerized production, design thinking for simplified logistics, and decreased demand for civil works.
(vi)   Modular scalability to increase the deployment speed of CO_2 capture equipment. It is possible to invest in partial capture right away and increase the capture capacity at a later stage.

The technology is compact and lightweight and allows for CO_2 capture from all industrial emission points (Figure 5). The modular, scalable, and mass-produced units give low cost per ton of CO_2 captured even at small-sized points of emission (50,000–100,000 tons CO_2/year). Modularization can also capture from larger points of emission such as fossil power.

Related costs

The upfront investment will depend on the point of emission. CCC aims for up to 50% reduction in CAPEX compared to conventional technology on points of emissions from 50,000–600,000 tons CO_2/year.

Operation costs will depend on access and cost of heat and cooling water, and choice of solvent. CCC believes that its higher freedom of choice on choosing solvents will reduce operating expenses compared to conventional technology. Tests are executed on both high concentrations of conventional amine-based solvents (+70% weight concentration) as well as on non-aqueous solvents.

The costs per ton of CO_2 captured will depend on the concentration of CO_2 in the flue gas. This is the same for every capture technology. Leaner flue gas requires more treatment to remove CO_2. As an example, capturing 90% from a 10% CO_2 concentrated flue gas will emit 1% CO_2 after capture. Capturing 90% from a 4% concentrated flue gas will emit 0.4% CO_2 after capture. This equates to a 96% capture on a 10% concentration. This will likely be competitive against conventional technology

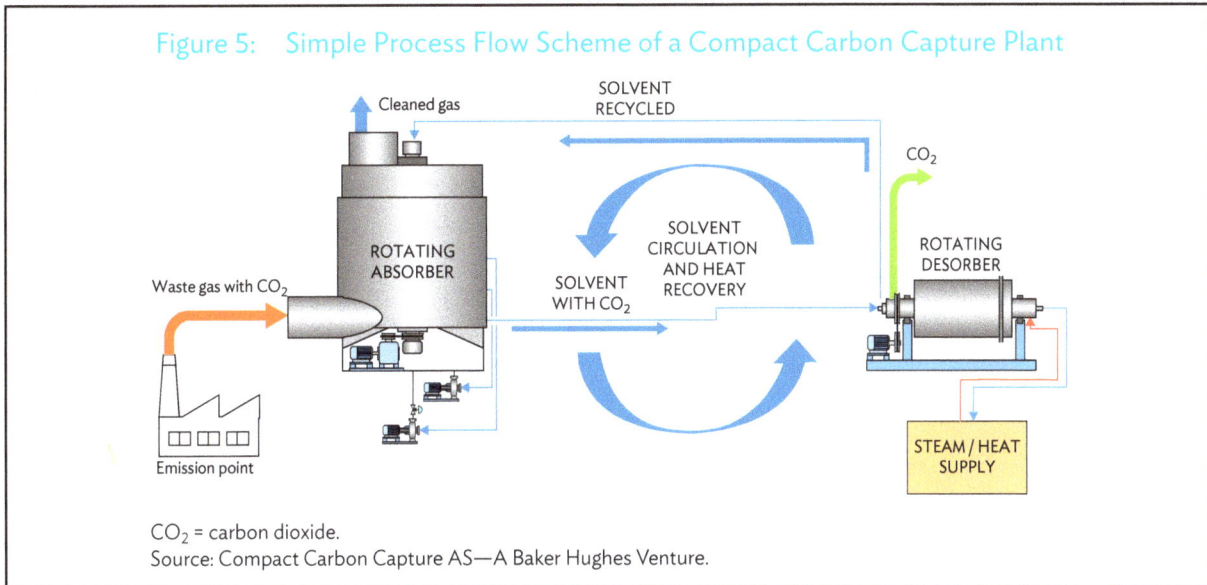

Figure 5:   Simple Process Flow Scheme of a Compact Carbon Capture Plant

CO_2 = carbon dioxide.
Source: Compact Carbon Capture AS—A Baker Hughes Venture.

on large points of emission and outcompete these on smaller emission points, as CAPEX will be a more significant part of the overall costs when tons captured over equipment lifetime will be fewer.

Potential application in Asia and other regions

This technology is highly relevant for implementation all over Asia. Potential markets can include the following:

(i)   **Existing power plants or large emission sources are not designed to be CCS ready.** Almost all large emission sources are designed without considering CCS. Available space is often a constraint for such projects to implement CCUS.

(ii) **Urban areas.** Compact Carbon Capture's technology can utilize non-toxic solvents to prevent the risk of releasing hazardous emissions from the capture process.

(iii) **Maritime sector.** CO_2 capture onboard ship traffic within, to, and from Asia.

(iv) **Fossil power plants.** Smaller units such as offshore and/or fossil can provide backup power for renewable energy plants.

Compact Carbon Capture and Baker Hughes together can provide local presence for service and maintenance.

Status and next steps

CCC is currently testing to qualify for technology readiness level-5 at an approximately 7 tons per day capacity plant. The next step is to build a 30 tons per day plant and demonstrate performance on industrial flue gas. Letters of intent have been received from (among others) Equinor and Total EP. A feasibility study for CO_2 capture onboard ships may also be performed as the low size/weight enables capture offshore.

Challenges in scale-up and deployment

CCC has developed an in-house white-box modeling tool that allows for accurate calculations for upscaling, and Baker Hughes provides additional experience and competence for designing plants suitable for mass production. Multiple tests for finding optimal solvents will be performed, as the CCC technology allows for high viscosity solvents and conventional data cannot be relied on.

Technology provider background

Compact Carbon Capture AS is a Baker Hughes Venture established in 2018 to commercialize the CCC technology developed from 2008 to 2020. The company owns and controls the technology, and partners with Baker Hughes to produce, install, and provide service and maintenance on the products. It is headquartered in Bergen, Norway but is represented globally through Baker Hughes. The team consists of highly qualified technical experts, and is headed by commercialization professionals. The company partners in development include—among others—Baker Hughes, Equinor, Fjell Technology Group, Prototech, and SINTEF.

Contact person:
Torleif Madsen (Product Manager)
E-mail: torleif.madsen@bakerhughes.com
Phone: +47 920 43 429

Suggestion for further reading

Compact Carbon Capture. 2019.
www.compactcarbon.com.

Direct Air Carbon Capture Storage

Technology provider
Carbon Infinity

Technology description
Direct air capture (DAC) systems require a steady flow of air—usually delivered via large fans—to come into contact with a filter. From this point, there are two commonly used methods by which to capture CO_2: chemical absorption and physical adsorption. Chemical absorption uses a liquid solvent—usually a caustic solvent—which absorbs CO_2 from ambient air to create a compound that is then heated, producing a highly pure gaseous stream of CO_2. Physical adsorption uses a solid sorbent—commonly metal-organic frameworks, zeolites, or other membrane technologies—in a process of chemisorption. CO_2 is adsorbed and desorbed from the solid sorbent using either heat, pressure, or moisture in a cyclical adsorption-desorption process.

Technology highlights and advantages

(i) CO_2 stream of 99.0%–99.9% purity can be produced for subsequent utilization or storage.
(ii) Can be used to abate emissions from mobile sources—such as aviation or shipping—of which there are currently limited available options.

Related costs

(i) Capital costs of a facility with a capture capacity of 1 million tons/year (t/y) of CO_2 are expected to be in the region of $500 million.
(ii) Cost per ton of CO_2 captured is estimated to range $200–$400 in 2020, falling to $100 between 2025 and 2030.

Potential application in Asia and other regions

(i) DAC technology has applications in the decarbonization of heavy industry and transportation—including cement production—shipping, and aviation.
(ii) Captured CO_2 can be transformed into high-value carbon-based products including synthetic fuels, carbon nanotubes, and CO_2-enriched concrete, closing the carbon cycle and powering the energy and industrial economy toward a carbon negative future.

Status and next steps

(i) Carbon Infinity is developing a modular physical adsorption capture technology that removes carbon dioxide from the air and converts this harmful greenhouse gas into carbon neutral transportation fuels and industrial products.
(ii) Progressing from the research and development and pilot testing stage, Carbon Infinity is seeking partnerships with government and industry to demonstrate the commercial viability of DAC technology in Asia.

Challenges in scale-up and deployment
The main obstacles to the development of a widespread DAC industry lie in

---

Box 4: Carbon Infinity Direct Air Carbon Capture Storage Key Features

Technology Highlights

- CO_2 stream of up to 99.9% purity

Development Stage

- Pilot demonstration

Sectors of Application

- Transportation
- Industries
- Negative emission solutions

(i)   policy initiatives to drive commercial interest in the sector,

(ii)   the deployment of financial capital to continue advancing the technology and drive carbon capture costs down further, and

(iii)   the introduction of true carbon pricing to reflect the environmental and social cost of emissions.

Policy initiatives like that introduced by the United States in 2019—known as "45Q"—have garnered a lot of interest by those across the CCS industry and beyond through the offer of tax credits of $35/t–$50/t for captured CO_2 to be utilized—such as enhanced oil recovery, synthetic fuels—or permanently sequestered. However, policy initiatives on this financial scale may not be feasible for countries with limited fiscal capacity, where other policy and regulatory measures ought to be implemented.

As the industry approaches commercialization, there is increasing interest from private and commercial groups in investing and financing the advanced development of DAC technology companies. This by no means suggests that public finance does not have a role to play, especially as most companies developing this technology have received public finance in one form or another. Public capital has a significant role to play, especially considering the long-term nature of returns from investment in capital intensive sectors like direct air capture and CCS.

Technology provider background

Carbon Infinity was founded in 2019 by a team of experts at Shanghai Jiao Tong University to commercialize research into direct air carbon capture technology. The primary product of Carbon Infinity is a comprehensive facility enabling the capture of CO_2 directly from the air for subsequent utilization as carbon-neutral transportation fuels or storage in saline aquifers. This award-winning technology by Carbon Infinity has been recognized by the Abu Dhabi government, and there are ongoing discussions with authorities across Asia to bring the technology to market.

Contact person:
David Izikowitz
E-mail: david@carboninfinity.com

Suggestions for further reading

- Carbon Infinity. https://carboninfinity.com/.
- National Academies of Sciences, Engineering, and Medicine. 2019. *Negative Emissions Technologies and Reliable Sequestration: A Research Agenda.* Washington, DC: The National Academies Press. https://doi.org/10.17226/25259.

Game-Changing Carbon Dioxide Utilization Technologies

Electro Methanol

Technology provider
Liquid Wind AB (Liquid Wind)

Technology description
Liquid Wind integrates proven technologies from its network of strategic partners to capture waste carbon dioxide and combine this with hydrogen generated from electrolyzers, to create a renewable methanol electrofuel (eMethanol). This process is powered by renewable energy from a wind farm (Figure 6).

Electrofuels, which are also called power-to-liquid fuels, are an emerging class of carbon-neutral drop-in replacement fuels, blendable with conventional petroleum products, which are made by storing electrical energy from renewable production as either liquid or gaseous fuels. This is an umbrella term for carbon-based fuels such as methane or methanol which are produced from CO_2 and water using electricity as the primary energy source. To differentiate from other sources, methanol produced in this way is referred to as eMethanol. Biofuels and electrofuels offer strongly viable alternatives for providing carbon neutral fuels to large and very large vessels.

Figure 6:   Process Diagram of eMethanol Production

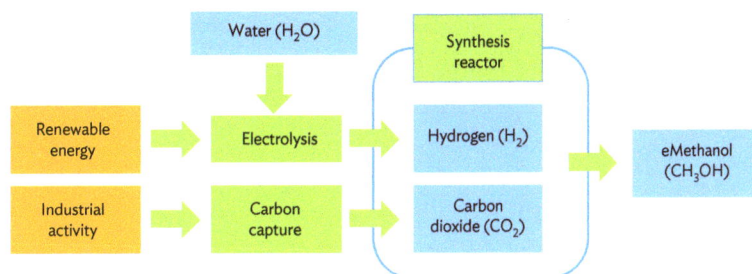

Source: Liquid Wind AB.

Technology highlights and advantages

(i) eMethanol production and utilization creates a carbon neutral loop as the CO_2 released from burning the eMethanol is captured and offset from industrial activities in the production of eMethanol. Renewable energy sources are used to power the reaction.

(ii) Each facility can prevent the emission of 100,000 tons of fossil CO_2 per year.

(iii) Each facility will convert 70,000 t per year of CO_2 into 50,000 t per year of eMethanol, supporting an industrial transition to a clean and/or circular economy.

(iv) The price will initially be on par with other clean fuel alternatives. It will be at a premium compared to conventional methanol and fossil fuels. However, emission reduction targets are increasing, and the scope of the emission trading scheme is expected to expand. This—combined with decreasing raw material costs and increasing process efficiency—means that eMethanol is expected to reach price parity with fossil fuels by 2030.

(v) eMethanol helps in the realization of a zero-pollution ambition (Figure 7). Methanol as a fuel emits 95% less particulate matter, 99% less sulfur oxide, and 70% less nitrogen oxide than Maritime Gasoline. eMethanol based on renewable energy and CO_2 from a biogenic source reduces CO_2 emissions by about 90%.

Potential application in Asia and other regions

Liquid Wind will scale up its operations based on a standard engineering model and licensed development package. The initial phase during 2020–2023 will be used to standardize the engineering model and build 2–3 facilities (Figure 8). During the 2024–2030 scale-up, 10+ more facilities will be directly developed, and 20+ developed through co-development with partners around the world. Liquid Wind aims to reach 500 facilities by 2050 through licensed development packages for local developers.

By standardizing the engineering model, Liquid Wind will be able to reduce the cost of the development package by 50% by 2023. Reducing the production cost of eMethanol equipment will play a significant role in reducing the cost of the development package.

Liquid Wind foresees learning curve-based cost reductions for integration, carbon capture, and electrolysis technology based on increased efficiency and economies of scale as global production of these technologies is ramped up. For the main cost component—renewable electricity—it is essential to locate the eMethanol facilities in low-price areas with high penetration of renewables (wind, photovoltaic). Another factor that can drive down the price under power purchase agreements is to aim for longer terms of 15 to 25 years. The long-term goal for Liquid Wind is to reach fossil parity for eMethanol from 2030 onwards.

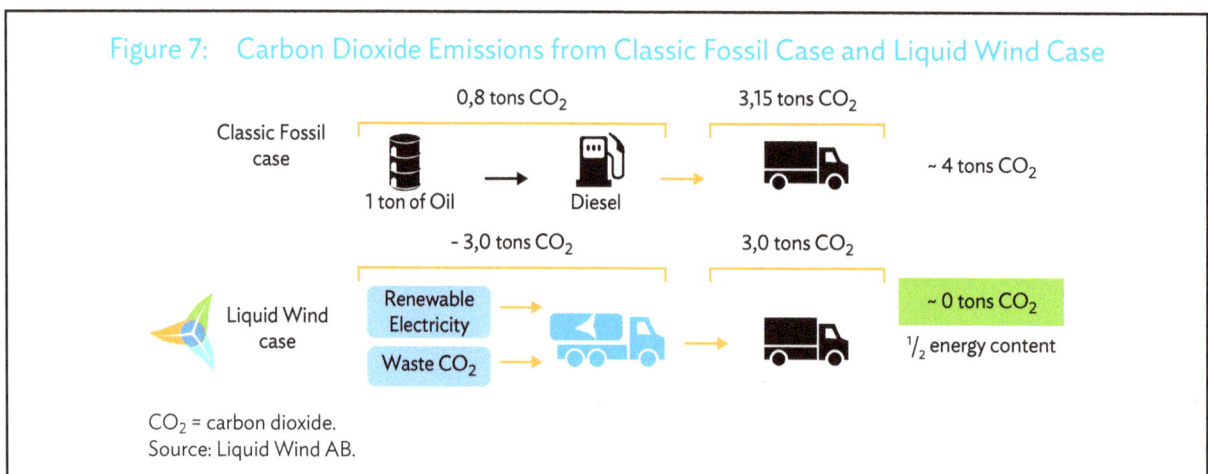

Figure 7: Carbon Dioxide Emissions from Classic Fossil Case and Liquid Wind Case

CO_2 = carbon dioxide.
Source: Liquid Wind AB.

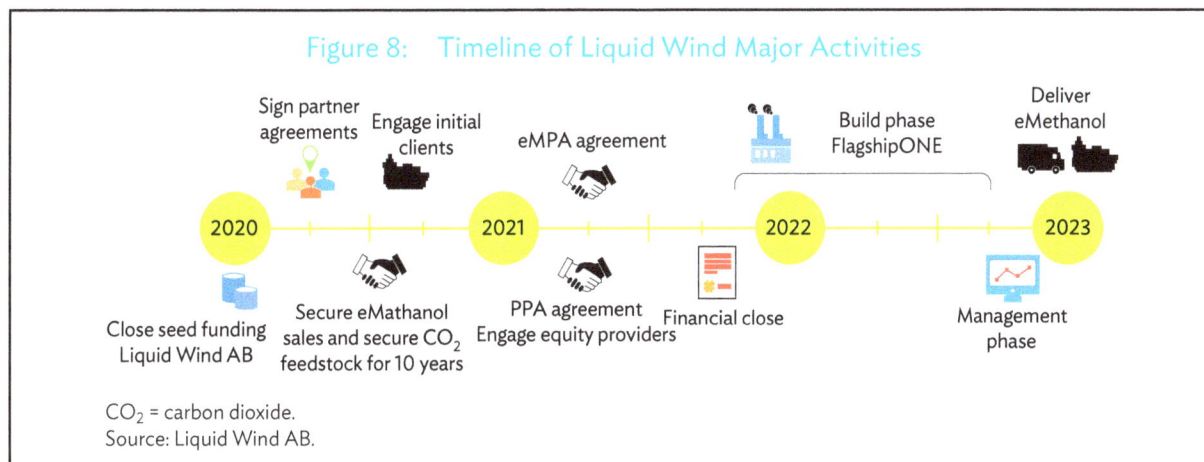

Figure 8:   Timeline of Liquid Wind Major Activities

CO_2 = carbon dioxide.
Source: Liquid Wind AB.

Status and next steps

The basic engineering and financial structuring of FacilityONE will start by November 2020. At financial close in early 2022, Liquid Wind will generate its first development revenue. For the construction of the eMethanol facility, Liquid Wind will engage a bankable engineering, procurement, and construction contractor guaranteeing the construction of the facility, on time, and on budget.

Challenges in scale-up and deployment

Blended financing with investor partners and the development company is essential to raise sufficient funding for developing and commissioning the first facility. Maturing this technology is a capital-intensive exercise. Liquid Wind has multiple letters of intent in place to finalize the input and output contracts for the first facility, but these are conditional on Liquid Wind developing the basic engineering packages and operational platform to finalize the first development package.

Technology provider background

Liquid Wind is a privately held company that was founded in 2017. It has eight full-time staff with complementary skills in business, finance, chemical engineering, and plant design. It has generated partnerships with world-leading technology providers (Nel Hydrogen, COWI, Carbon Clean Solutions, Haldor Topsoe, and Siemens), as well as major plant operators and CO_2 suppliers in the pulp and paper industry. It has also secured the interest of major eMethanol purchasers such as Stena Line, Royal Caribbean, A.P Möller-Maersk, Marinvest, and Ford Motors.

Contact Person:
Tuya Bold
Head of Finance
E-mail: Tuya@liquidwind.se

Suggestion for further reading

J. Ovcina. 2020. *The Power-to-Fuel project wants to convert CO_2 into carbon-neutral fuel.* Offshore Energy. 27 March. https://www.offshore-energy.biz/the-power-to-fuel-project-wants-to-convert-co2-into-carbon-neutral-fuel/.

Econic Catalyst Technology for Utilization of Carbon Dioxide as a Feedstock for the Polyurethane Industry

Technology provider

Econic Technologies Limited (Econic)

Technology description

The proprietary catalyst technology of Econic allows for recycled carbon dioxide (CO_2) emissions to be used as a feedstock in polyol manufacture. In the first market application, recycled CO_2 is incorporated into a range of polyols—the building blocks of polyurethanes—substituting up to 50% of the conventional fossil-based feedstocks, propylene oxide and/or ethylene oxide. Econic technology produces polyols with tunable amounts of incorporated CO_2, which have enhanced performances that are tailored for specific applications. Beyond polyols, Econic technology has been proven to deliver the same CO_2 benefits in the surfactant, lubricant, and high molecular weight polymer sectors.

Technology highlights and advantages

Econic catalyst technology allows for the substitution of up to 50% of conventional oil-based feedstocks with CO_2 with applications across a range of industries (Figure 9). Its first target market is in the manufacture of polyols, the building blocks of polyurethane materials. Life-cycle assessment studies indicate that polyols produced with average CO_2 contents (25%–35%) will have reduced CO_2 emissions footprints in the order of 25%–40%. Across the global polyurethanes market, a 30% adoption of Econic

---

Box 6: Econic Catalyst Key Features

Technology Highlights

- Creates tunable polyols using recycled CO_2
- Allows replacement of up to 50% of oil-based raw materials with low-cost CO_2

Development Stage

- Commercialization

Sector of Application

- Chemical industry, specifically polyurethanes

Figure 9: Cost Comparison of Polymer Made Using Conventional Catalysts and Econic Catalysts

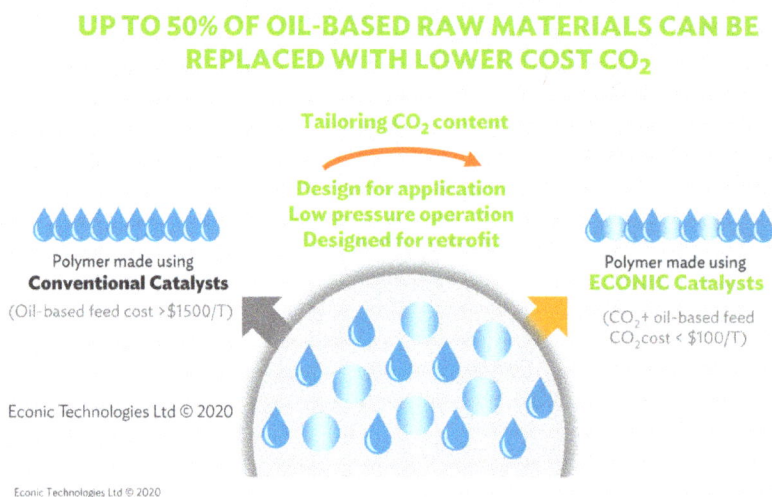

UP TO 50% OF OIL-BASED RAW MATERIALS CAN BE REPLACED WITH LOWER COST CO_2

Tailoring CO_2 content

Design for application
Low pressure operation
Designed for retrofit

Polymer made using
Conventional Catalysts
(Oil-based feed cost >$1500/T)

Polymer made using
ECONIC Catalysts
(CO_2+ oil-based feed
CO_2 cost < $100/T)

Econic Technologies Ltd © 2020

Econic Technologies Ltd © 2020

CO_2 = carbon dioxide, T = metric ton.
Source: Econic Technologies Limited.

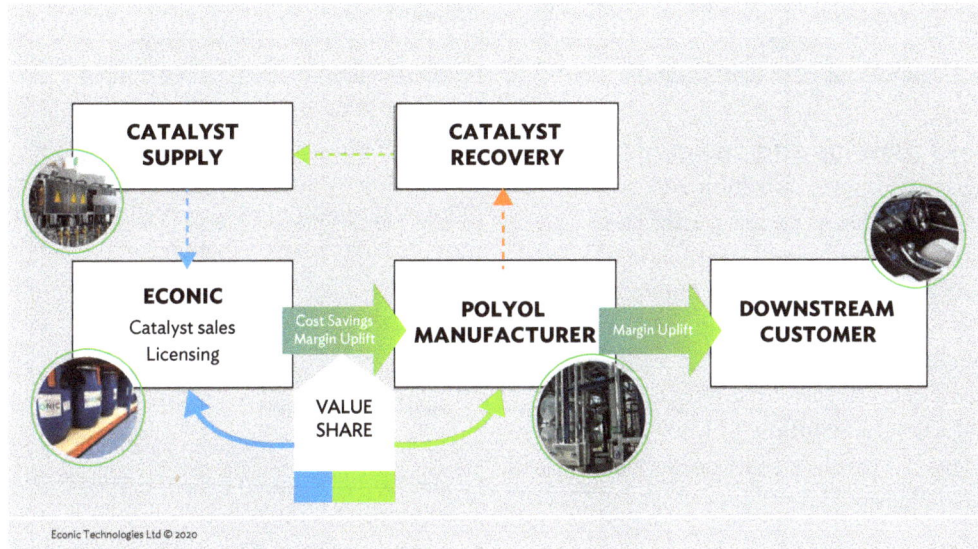

Figure 10:   Overview of the Econic Supply Chain

Source: Econic Technologies Limited.

catalyst technology could result in the consumption and prevention of 5 million tons of CO_2 emissions per year. Polyols created by the Econic system can be utilized in all aspects of the polyurethane market, from housing insulation to car interiors to running shoes and refrigerators.

The Econic system incorporates CO_2 into polyols using less energy than the existing industrial process, and—compared to competing technologies—is the only system that facilitates bespoke incorporation of CO_2 into products, thereby optimizing production and end-product performance. Furthermore, it does so under the same equipment and processing conditions of existing production facilities, allowing fast, simple, and low-cost adoption by retrofit.

Beyond polyols, the same utilization of CO_2 has been demonstrated in the surfactant, lubricant, and high molecular weight polymer sectors, dramatically increasing the scale of carbon benefit the Econic technology can deliver.

Related costs

Rather than providing sustainability at a cost, Econic technology increases product margins for polyol producers by reducing raw material and operating costs, while also increasing product performance and product value. All of this is achieved through the utilization of waste CO_2, resulting in a more profitable and sustainable business for the user. Adoption for the user is achieved through a simple, low-cost retrofit to existing facilities, along with the supply of a technology license and ongoing catalyst sales from Econic (Figure 10).

Potential application in Asia and other regions

Polyol production and consumption are global industries, with 50% of global polyol consumption occurring within Asia. Polyol products produced with the Econic system can be utilized across all sectors of the polyurethane industry, including rigid foams (housing, construction, and refrigeration insulation), flexible foams (bedding, car seating, shoe soles) and coatings, elastomers, sealants, and adhesives.

Status and next steps

Production of the system catalyst has been demonstrated successfully at substantial scale. The performance of materials utilizing Econic CO_2 polyols have been demonstrated across all sectors of the polyurethane industry, and key performance improvements have been seen in all applications. Strong interest has been expressed by many major global chemical producers, and evaluations of the system are progressing to large pilot scale at clients' sites in Europe and Asia in 2021 before full commercialization.

Challenges in scale-up and deployment

Key challenges to commercialization include access to influencers within key potential customers to drive the pace of adoption of the technology within the traditionally conservative chemical industry. Whilst not essential, legislation that would encourage the industry to adopt carbon utilization technologies—like that of Econic's—would help accelerate adoption, as would regional or global financial incentives that support climate change technologies.

Technology provider background

Econic was established in 2012 by Charlotte Williams (CSO) and Mike Kember (Head of Research and Intellectual Property) as a result of discoveries made as part of the PhD thesis of M. Kember at Imperial College, London. Econic is a high-value catalyst technology business that allows the recycling of low-cost CO_2 to displace high-cost petrochemical feedstocks and is currently operating in the polyols (polyurethane) market.

Since 2012 the business has grown to about 30 employees, has relocated from London to Cheshire, and is developing both the catalyst and associated process technology to market readiness with the help of—among others—noted investors IP Group and OGCI Climate Investments. The technology is now at the brink of full commercialization within the global polyurethanes industry and poised to access wider market opportunities beyond this sector.

Suggestions for further reading

- Econic Technologies. 2017. www.econic-technologies.com.
- Econic Technologies Ltd. 2020. LinkedIn. https://www.linkedin.com/company/econic-technologies-limited/.
- Econic Technologies. 2020. @Econictech. Twitter. https://twitter.com/econictech?lang=en.
- Econic Technologies. 2019. YouTube. *Turning CO2 into endless potential.* https://www.youtube.com/watch?v=hCwqd21G_LA&t=173s. 16 December.

LanzaTech Gas Fermentation Process

Technology provider
LanzaTech

Technology description
The LanzaTech process converts carbon-rich gas streams to valuable products using its proprietary microbes that feed on gases (rather than sugars, as in traditional fermentation). The LanzaTech microbe occurs naturally and has been optimized to economically produce ethanol and enable economic routes to jet fuel and high-value chemicals from a variety of carbon-rich gas streams, such as

(i)   industrial off-gases from steel and ferroalloy mills;
(ii)   petroleum refineries, petrochemical complexes, and gas processing facilities;
(iii)   syngas generated from any biomass resource, including municipal solid waste, organic industrial waste, and agricultural waste;
(iv)   reformed biogas and landfill gas; and
(v) CO_2 off-gas from biorefineries.

By capturing the carbon contained in these gas streams, the LanzaTech gas fermentation technology platform enables the production of low carbon fuels and chemicals to serve as building blocks for indispensable consumer products such as rubber, plastics, and synthetic fibers. LanzaTech estimates that its products reduce greenhouse gas emissions by at least 70% when compared to equivalent products derived from fresh fossil resources.

LanzaTech ethanol is chemically identical to other forms of ethanol and can be used as a fuel as well as an ingredient in other consumer goods. The ethanol can also be converted to ethylene—which is one of the most commonly produced organic chemicals—using established commercially available technology. Ethylene is widely used in the production of polyethylene which is a raw material in the production of plastic products.

Box 7: LanzaTech Gas Fermentation Process Key Features

Technology Highlights

- Converts carbon-rich waste gases to various chemicals
- Reduces industry carbon emissions while producing building block chemicals
- Produces fuels with greenhouse gas emissions that are at least 70% lower than gasoline

Development Stage

- Commercialization

Sectors of Application

- Petroleum and gas processing
- Steel and ferroalloy industries
- Waste to energy
- Fuels
- Chemical industries (including rubber, plastics, synthetic fibers)

Technology highlights and advantages
By capturing the carbon contained in waste gas streams, the LanzaTech gas fermentation process reduces industry carbon emissions whilst producing products that serve as building blocks for indispensable consumer goods such as rubber, plastics, and synthetic fibers.

Environmental assessments of the LanzaTech process have been performed in cooperation with Michigan Technological University, the Roundtable on Sustainable Biomaterials (RSB), E4Tech, Ecofys, and Tsinghua University. These studies have shown that by using waste gases that would otherwise be combusted and emitted as CO_2 and pollutants, the LanzaTech gas fermentation process can produce fuels with greenhouse gas emissions at least 70% lower than gasoline. Not only does the LanzaTech process offer the opportunity to reduce the greenhouse gas footprint of transportation fuels, but it can also reduce local air pollutants such as particulate and nitrogen oxide emissions by as much as 80% or more.

The robustness of the LanzaTech microbial system enables it to use a variety of point-sourced, nonfood, low-cost, and highly abundant feedstocks. Gas fermentation can utilize feedstocks ranging from carbon monoxide (CO) to CO_2-rich waste streams: CO can provide both carbon and energy for the organism; CO_2 only provides carbon which means a source of chemical energy, hydrogen (H_2), must be added for CO_2 conversion. In a CO-rich stream, the organism can make the H_2 it needs from water, making CO waste streams of various compositions ideal for gas fermentation. The conversion to ethanol is stoichiometric and the organism can use any combination of CO, H_2, or CO_2, provided there is sufficient energy. The technology can be deployed to convert various pockets of waste industrial carbon and solid waste carbon residues including waste biomass, black liquor from the pulp and paper sector, and municipal solid waste as shown in Figure 11.

Waste gas streams comprised primarily of CO_2 need an additional energy source. CO_2 electrolysis can produce CO using electricity to provide the energy required for the chemical reduction. Alternatively, electrolysis can be used to produce H_2 from water; the hydrogen can be used to convert CO_2 directly via gas fermentation. Gas fermentation technologies are positioned to take advantage of the expected continued price reductions and capacity increases for renewable electricity maximizing utilization of CO_2 streams by developing and integrating these approaches.

When using municipal solid waste, the process avoids the need to landfill or incinerate unsorted, unrecyclable waste streams, avoiding both methane and CO_2 emissions. These feedstock gases can alternatively be used to generate electricity, but this is generally done at low efficiency and can also come from 100% renewable resources today. The LanzaTech process thus supports the transition to a fully renewable grid and produces fewer pollutants such as particulate emissions and nitrogen oxide than power from incineration technologies.

Today ethanol can be made from sugar fermentation or via petrochemical processes, using crude oil. By using wastes and residues for ethanol production, fossil resources, land, and food crops are avoided.

Synthetic biology has enabled LanzaTech a broad and diverse product portfolio (Figure 12). While the LanzaTech microbe naturally produces ethanol, a broader spectrum of new products is possible with modifications to the microbe's genetic structure.

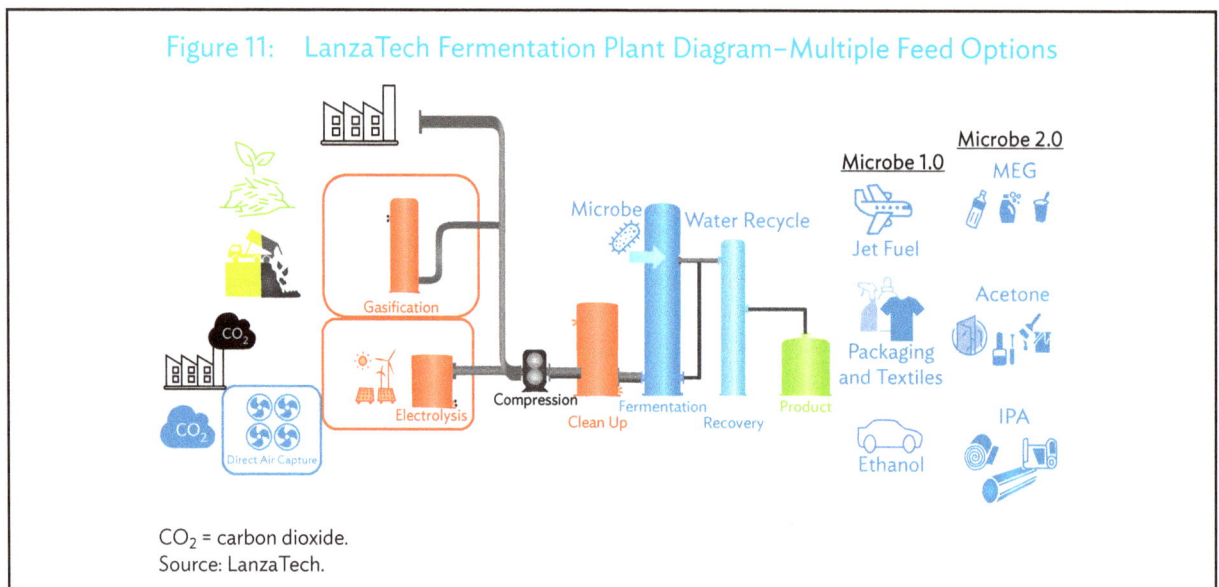

Figure 11:   LanzaTech Fermentation Plant Diagram–Multiple Feed Options

CO_2 = carbon dioxide.
Source: LanzaTech.

Figure 12: LanzaTech Product Streams

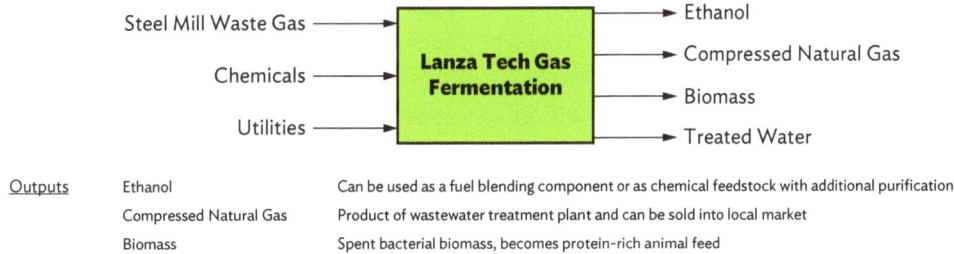

Inputs		Process	Outputs
Steel Mill Waste Gas →		**Lanza Tech Gas Fermentation**	→ Ethanol
Chemicals →			→ Compressed Natural Gas
Utilities →			→ Biomass
			→ Treated Water

Outputs		
	Ethanol	Can be used as a fuel blending component or as chemical feedstock with additional purification
	Compressed Natural Gas	Product of wastewater treatment plant and can be sold into local market
	Biomass	Spent bacterial biomass, becomes protein-rich animal feed

Source: LanzaTech.

LanzaTech has developed the capability to switch products at a commercial scale within a matter of weeks. This capability will enable LanzaTech customers to maximize the value of their assets by producing the highest value product at any given time. Because this capability is unique to LanzaTech for gas fermenting microbes, LanzaTech has several collaborations with end users targeting the production of new molecules.

Related costs

A LanzaTech facility derives revenues from several products such as ethanol from biogas and spent bacterial biomass that can be sold as protein-rich animal feed. Geographic location will impact the economics of a project due to several factors including cost of utilities such as water and grid electricity for process power, cost of labor and materials during construction, labor during operation, market conditions, and available incentives for fuel production. The type of feed gas used will also impact the economics with richer feed gas streams giving greater yields of product. The upfront investment ranges from \$1,500/t to \$5,500/t ethanol capacity (lower end for typical scale projects or use of industrial waste gases; higher end for small scale projects that also include gasification of solid wastes and high-cost locations) and the full cost of production—including the capital—ranges from \$500/t to \$1,000/t, depending on the capacity, feedstock, and scope of the project. The cost per ton of CO_2 diverted is less than zero as there is a net profit for the operation for each ton of CO_2 avoided.

Potential application in Asia and the world

The LanzaTech Gas Fermentation Process applies to multiple sectors in Asia and the rest of the world. LanzaTech uses a variety of waste gases to produce chemicals that serve as building blocks to indispensable consumer products such as fuels, rubber, plastics, and synthetic fibers. Sources of waste gases include the refinery, steel, and ferroalloy emissions, as well as gases derived from unsorted, unrecyclable municipal solid waste (household waste) and agricultural residues.

Status and next steps

LanzaTech technology has been demonstrated at five industrial sites with over 50,000 hours of operation using steel mill waste gases, and approximately 50,000 hours using syngas from municipal solid waste gasification. To develop and scale its economic gas fermentation process, LanzaTech has developed an integrated technology platform including expertise in synthetic biology, process optimization, and bioreactor design. In addition to the customer-owned pilot and/or demonstration units, LanzaTech operates a research and development and piloting facility in Soperton, Georgia known as LanzaTech Freedom Pines Biorefinery.

With the success of its pilot and demonstration programs, LanzaTech has entered commercialization. The first commercial plant started up in the People's Republic of China in May 2018 and has produced over 74 million liters of fuel-grade ethanol from steel mill emissions while diverting over 100,000 t of CO_2 from the atmosphere as of November 2020. LanzaTech is developing a pipeline of commercial projects that extends well beyond steel off-gas and ethanol product applications.

Challenges in scale-up and deployment

Utilization of a variety of feedstocks is crucial to long term, sustainable growth. The robustness of the LanzaTech microbial system enables it to use a variety of feedstocks. LanzaTech is currently deploying its technology in the steel, ferroalloy, and refining sectors while working with partners to develop projects using syngas produced from gasified biomass and municipal solid waste. Continuing to develop projects based on these additional feedstocks is critical to maximize the deployment of the technology and maximize greenhouse gas savings. Conducting commercial feasibility studies for these project opportunities is generally one of the critical needs to enable projects to proceed. LanzaTech feedstock gases all have the advantage of being point-source, nonfood, low-cost, and highly abundant. The total global potential ethanol production from these various feedstocks is greater than 2.4 trillion liters per year.

Technology provider background

LanzaTech is a global leader in gas fermentation technology. Gas fermentation uses a living, naturally occurring organism to ferment gases to make fuels—such as ethanol—and chemicals, similar to the traditional fermentation of sugars to make alcohol, where yeast eats sugars to make beer.

LanzaTech was founded in New Zealand in 2005. Company locations include:

(i)   Corporate Headquarters and research and development in Chicago, Illinois, United States.
(ii)   Operations and business offices in the People's Republic of China and India.
(iii)   Facilities at Freedom Pines Biorefinery, Georgia, United States.

The company has approximately 200 staff globally and an intellectual property portfolio of >900 patents granted and >400 pending patents. Its key stakeholders include Novo Holdings, Khosla Ventures, Mitsui, Indian Oil Corporation, BASF, Petronas, Primetals, and Suncor. Its leadership team includes Jennifer Holmgren (CEO) and Sean Simpson (CSO and Founder).

Contact information:

United States:
Illinois Science and Technology Park
8045 Lamon Avenue
Suite 400
Skokie, Illinois 60077, US
+1-847-324-2400

People's Republic of China:
Room 1613, Shanghai Zhongrong Plaza
No. 1088 Pudong South Road, Pudong New District
Shanghai 200122, People's Republic of China
+86-21-80176500
+86-21-80176501

India:
LanzaTech Private Ltd
515-517, Spaze I-Tech Park, Sohna Road,
Gurgaon, Haryana, 122018, India
+91 124 4110520

Suggestion for further reading

LanzaTech. 2019. https://www.lanzatech.com/.

Osaki CoolGen Project: Integrated Coal Gasification Fuel Cell Combined Cycle

Technology Provider
Osaki CoolGen Corporation

Technology Description
The Osaki CoolGen Project consists of three demonstration steps: (i) oxygen-blown integrated coal gasification combined cycle (IGCC), (ii) oxygen-blown IGCC with carbon dioxide (CO_2) capture, and (iii) IGFC (IGCC with fuel cells) with CO_2 capture. IGFC could be the ultimate high-efficiency, electricity-generating technology, which combines gas turbine, steam turbine, and fuel cells. This project is the first in the world to demonstrate CO_2 capture technology from IGFC.

In the first step, coal is gasified in a gasifier to generate syngas with carbon monoxide (CO) and hydrogen (H_2) as the main components (Figure 13). After gasification, the heat of the syngas is recovered in a syngas cooler and a gas clean-up unit removes impurities and sulfur from the syngas. Next, the syngas is combusted in the gas turbine combustors to drive the gas turbine. The combustion exhaust gas in the gas turbine is emitted from the stack after having its heat recovered by a heat recovery steam generator. Meanwhile, the steam turbine is driven by steam generated in the syngas cooler and the heat recovery steam generator.

In the second step demonstrating oxygen-blown IGCC with CO_2 capture, part of the syngas after gas cleanup is sent to the added CO_2 capture unit. The shift reactor converts the CO in the syngas with steam (H_2O) into CO_2 and H_2. After that, only the CO_2 is captured in the CO_2 absorber. The syngas after the CO_2 capture becomes fuel gas rich in hydrogen and is then sent to the gas turbine.

With an IGFC with CO_2 capture, fuel cell modules—the basic structural unit of a solid oxide fuel cell (SOFC)—are lined up, and the hydrogen-rich gas after CO_2 separation is sent to the SOFC.

Technology highlights and advantages

(i) The commercialized IGFC is an ultimate-combined technology and a further enhancement of efficiency compared with the latest ultra-supercritical pulverized coal-fired thermal power (the mainstream of coal-fired thermal power in Japan).

(ii) The project aims to achieve a net thermal efficiency—higher heating value—of approximately 47% while capturing 90% of the CO_2 in a 500 megawatt-class commercial unit by combined IGFC with a CO_2 capture unit.

Related costs
Generation cost is equivalent to that of the latest commercial pulverized coal-fired plant in Japan.

Potential application in Asia and the world
IGCC and IGFC can help reduce CO_2 emissions and achieve global sustainable development by allowing the efficient use of low-cost coal to meet increased power demand. Furthermore, by combining these with CO_2 capture technology, high-efficiency and near-zero CO_2 emission coal-fired plants can be realized and recovered CO_2 can be used for CCUS.

Figure 13:   Osaki CoolGen Project Diagram

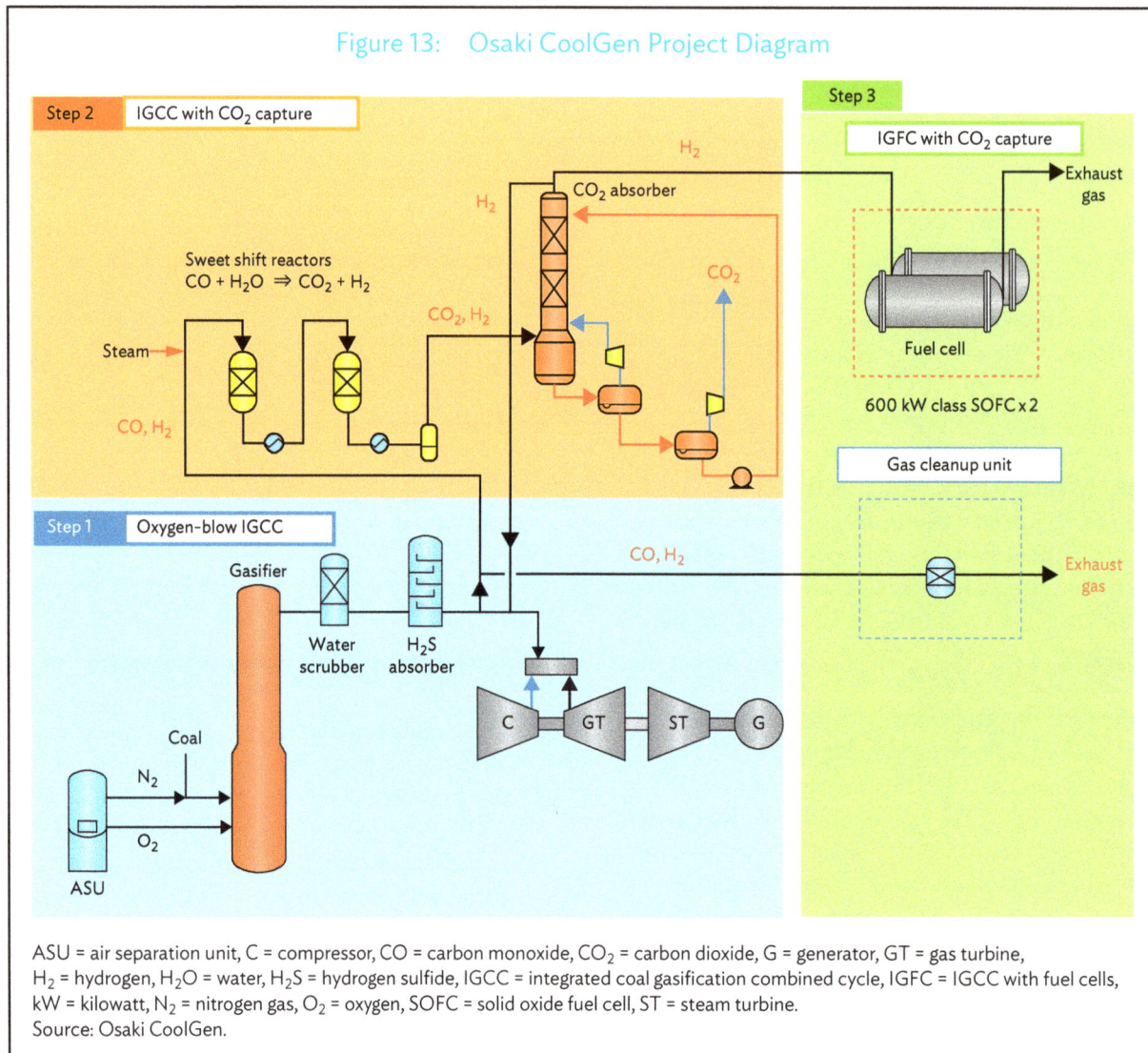

Step 2 — IGCC with CO_2 capture

Step 3 — IGFC with CO_2 capture

Sweet shift reactors
$CO + H_2O \Rightarrow CO_2 + H_2$

CO_2 absorber

H_2

H_2

CO_2, H_2

CO_2

CO, H_2

Steam

Fuel cell

600 kW class SOFC x 2

Gas cleanup unit

Step 1 — Oxygen-blow IGCC

Gasifier

Water scrubber

H_2S absorber

CO, H_2

Exhaust gas

Coal

N_2

O_2

ASU

C   GT   ST   G

Exhaust gas

ASU = air separation unit, C = compressor, CO = carbon monoxide, CO_2 = carbon dioxide, G = generator, GT = gas turbine, H_2 = hydrogen, H_2O = water, H_2S = hydrogen sulfide, IGCC = integrated coal gasification combined cycle, IGFC = IGCC with fuel cells, kW = kilowatt, N_2 = nitrogen gas, O_2 = oxygen, SOFC = solid oxide fuel cell, ST = steam turbine.
Source: Osaki CoolGen.

Status and next steps

The Osaki CoolGen Project is being implemented as a project assisted by the Ministry of Economy, Trade and Industry since April 2012 and by the New Energy and Industrial Technology Development Organization since April 2016.

The first step of the project has achieved its target of obtaining sufficient performance of an oxygen-blown IGCC, which is a core technology of the IGFC. The project timeline is shown in Figure 14.

Technology provider background

Osaki CoolGen Corporation was founded by the Chugoku Electric Power Co., Inc. and Electric Power Development Co., Ltd. aiming to achieve the establishment of IGFC with CO_2 capture—which is one of the ultimate high-efficiency technologies and CO_2 capture technology. The company was founded in 2009.

Figure 14:   Osaki CoolGen Project Timeline

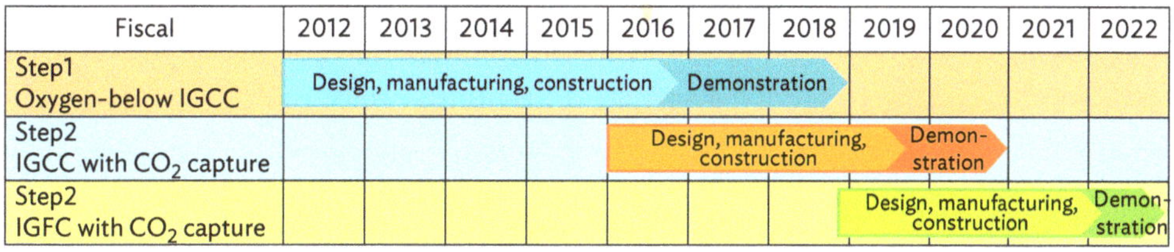

Fiscal	2012	2013	2014	2015	2016	2017	2018	2019	2020	2021	2022
Step1 Oxygen-below IGCC	Design, manufacturing, construction					Demonstration					
Step2 IGCC with CO_2 capture					Design, manufacturing, construction			Demon-stration			
Step2 IGFC with CO_2 capture								Design, manufacturing, construction			Demon-stration

CO_2 = carbon dioxide, IGCC = integrated coal gasification combined cycle, IGFC = IGCC with fuel cells.
Source: Osaki CoolGen.

Contact person/s:
Haruhito Kubota
Planning and Research Group Director
Tel.: +81 50 8201 0202
E-mail: kubota@osaki-coolgen.jp

Takehisa Okino
Staff Deputy Manager
General Affairs Department
Planning and Research Group
Tel.: +81 50 8201 0211
E-mail: okino@osaki-coolgen.jp

Suggestion for further reading
Osaki CoolGen Corporation. 2020. https://www.osaki-coolgen.jp/en/.

Allam-Fetvedt Cycle

Technology provider

NET Power and 8 Rivers
(The natural gas version of the cycle is being developed by NET Power LLC, while the biomass and coal version is being developed by 8 Rivers).

NET Power is a clean energy technology company with a proprietary process that generates lower-cost power with zero emissions. NET Power partners with developers and other stakeholders in commercializing its power system by providing carbon-free, affordable, and flexible power from natural gas. Its mission is to provide advanced clean energy to consumers worldwide by generating lower-cost power with zero emissions. The NET Power/8 Rivers Allam-Fetvedt Cycle promises the only immediately available technology that meets world climate goals without paying more for electricity.

Technology description

The Allam-Fetvedt (Allam) Cycle is a method of carbon capture, which 8 Rivers invented in 2009. The Allam Cycle burns gasified coal (Figure 15) or natural gas (Figure 16) in pure oxygen, rather than air. This creates a high purity stream of CO_2 at 300 bar and between 900°C and 1200°C. Instead of steam, this supercritical CO_2 is used to drive the turbine. The CO_2 can then be sent into the pipeline at no additional cost. CO_2 capture is inherent to the system, and selling CO_2 is a key source of revenue.

Multiple revenue streams give NET Power a cost advantage. By using supercritical CO_2 as a working fluid, this cycle can reach approximately the same efficiency as a conventional natural gas power plant while achieving over 97% carbon capture and creating zero air pollutants.

The Allam Cycle presents an opportunity not just for the electricity sector, but also for the oil and gas, environmental, and petrochemicals sectors. The technology could lower the cost of electricity from fossil fuels, while co-generating CO_2 for domestic enhanced oil recovery, cement production, and

Box 9: NET Power and 8 Rivers Allam-Fetvedt Cycle Key Features

Technology Highlights

- Able to reach 50%–>60% LHV efficiency inclusive of capturing 97% of the generated CO_2

Development Stage

- Commercialization

Sector of Application

- Power generation

other forms of carbon utilization, as well as for underground sequestration. It will co-produce other valuable gases, nitrogen, and argon, which support manufacturing.

Technology highlights and advantages

This differentiation is notable because the technology offers economic advantages and environmental benefits: zero emissions, lower power costs, a complement to renewables, multiple revenue streams, and a solution that is made for anywhere. This makes existing power plants economically and environmentally obsolete.

By providing reliable, low-cost, and flexible power with virtually no carbon emissions, the Allam Cycle is an excellent complement to growing wind and solar energy portfolios around the world. Each plant can provide >1,415 MWh in energy storage services by taking in excess renewable electricity, using it to create pure oxygen, and storing the oxygen in tanks for later use when the sun sets or the wind slows.

NET Power can reach 50%–>60% lower heating value (LHV) efficiency that captures 97% of the generated CO_2 at 150 bar pressure, which is at comparable efficiency to combined-cycle natural gas plants without carbon capture, and would save energy and cost compared to combined-cycle plants equipped with post-combustion capture given the parasitic load that would incur. With this capture

Figure 15: Allam Cycle Coal Diagram

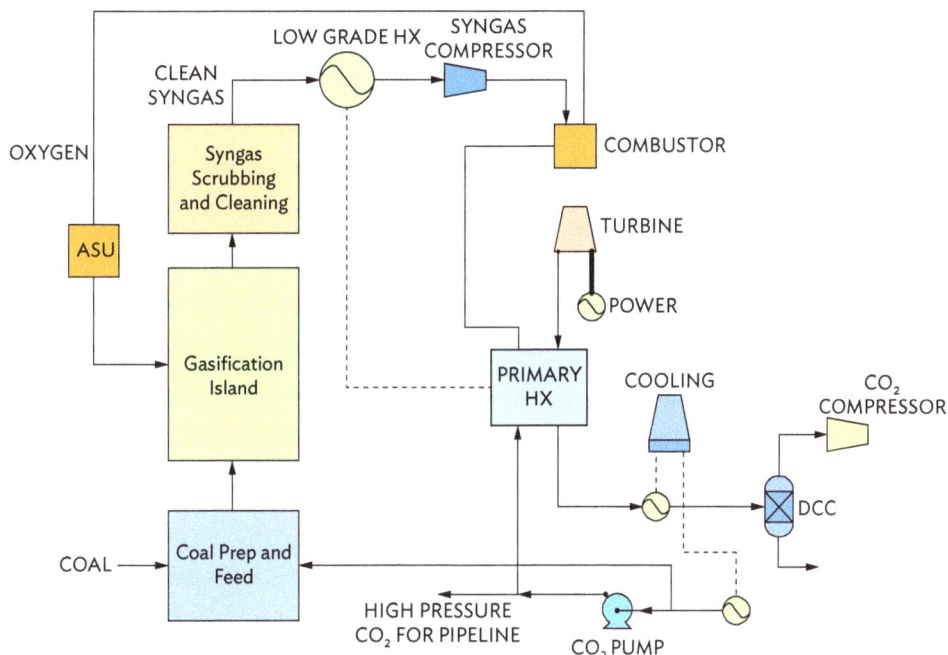

ASU = air separation unit, CO_2 = carbon dioxide, DCC = direct-contact cooling, HX = heat exchange.
Source: 8 Rivers.

Figure 16: Allam Cycle Natural Gas Diagram

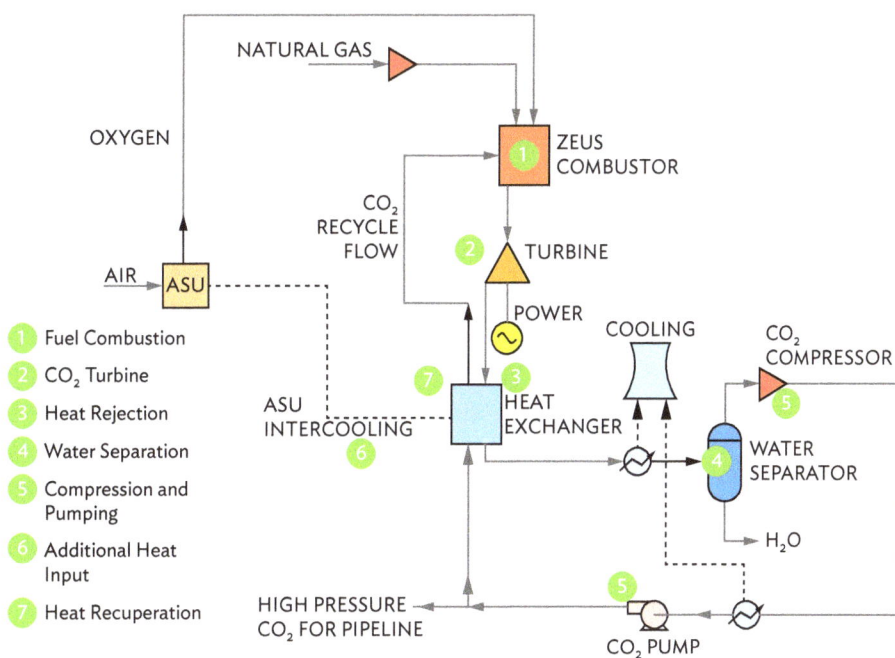

ASU = air separation unit, CO_2 = carbon dioxide, H_2O = water.
Source: NET Power LLC.

capacity, about 860,000 tons of CO_2 per year can be saved at a 280 megawatt (MW) output plant.

The Coal Allam Cycle can hit 42.25% LHV efficiency inclusive of capturing >93% of the generated CO_2 at 150 bar pressure. The average heat rate for a coal plant globally is 35% LHV, so the Coal Allam Cycle would be one of the most efficient coal plants available and would be the highest efficiency coal plant with high rates of carbon capture. The Coal Allam Cycle can capture and reduce about 1.6 million tons of CO_2 ($mtCO_2$)/per year at a 286 MW output plant. This same analysis would hold for gasified biomass with carbon capture.

Related costs

The levelized costs of the Allam Cycle on natural gas (Figure 17) and coal (Figure 18) are shown to be competitive with new combined-cycle plants.

Potential application in Asia and the world

This technology is a global solution, with multiple partners who are committed to meeting world 2050 climate goals. This partnership has over 418 NET Power-issued patents in more than 30 countries,

and an additional 246 Allam Cycle associated global patents (issued and pending).

The initial commercial NET Power plants are likely to be in the US, where there are substantial tax credits (Tax Code 45Q–Credit for carbon oxide sequestration), and over 8,000 km in CO_2 pipelines connecting over 100 CO_2 offtakes, expanding the map of locations to build a CCS plant with minimal infrastructure required. Nevertheless, multiple NET Power plants are in various stages of development worldwide. Global deployment of Allam Cycle could bring significant cost savings. With conservative industrial gas prices, this system will be cheaper than conventional coal with $15 CO_2 and at cost parity with $0 CO_2.

Locations where CO_2 gets the highest value will likely build the initial projects, getting the technology down the learning curve so it can compete without CO_2 revenue. Those locations include the Republic of Korea with its Emissions Trading Scheme, potential Asian enhanced oil recovery fields in the People's Republic of China, India, Indonesia, Malaysia, Viet Nam, as well as the United Arab Emirates.

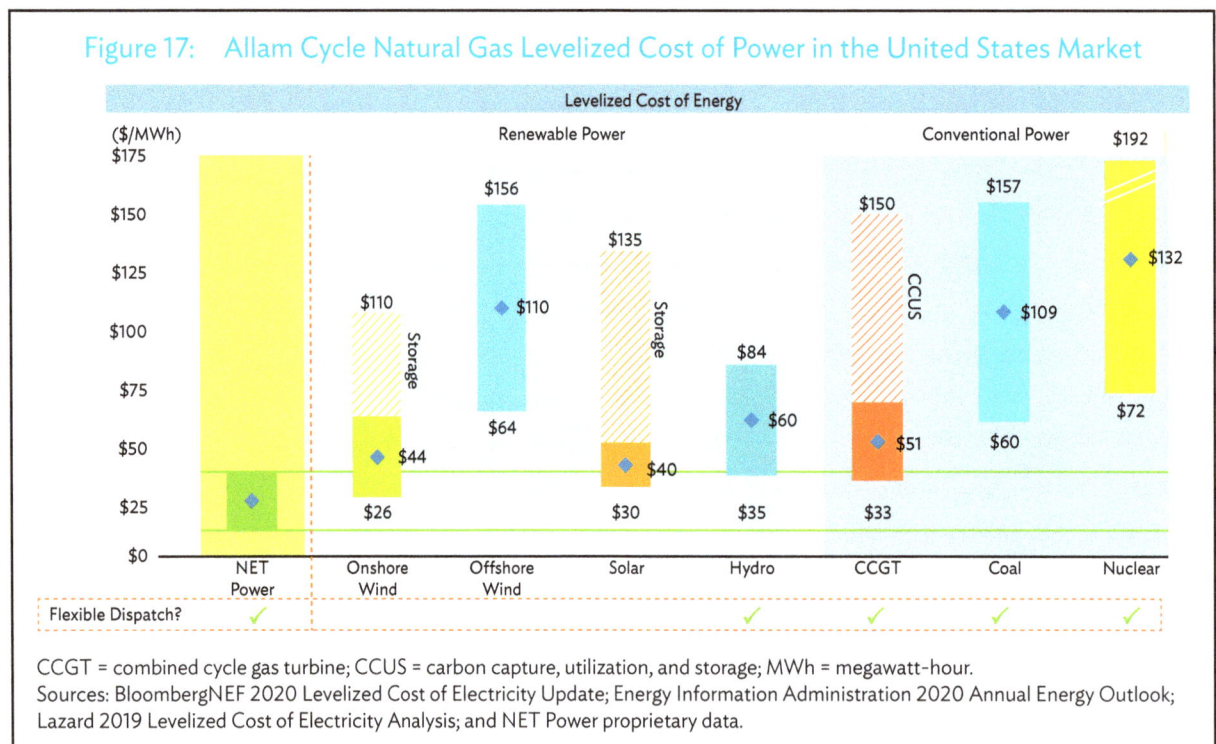

Figure 17:   Allam Cycle Natural Gas Levelized Cost of Power in the United States Market

CCGT = combined cycle gas turbine; CCUS = carbon capture, utilization, and storage; MWh = megawatt-hour.
Sources: BloombergNEF 2020 Levelized Cost of Electricity Update; Energy Information Administration 2020 Annual Energy Outlook; Lazard 2019 Levelized Cost of Electricity Analysis; and NET Power proprietary data.

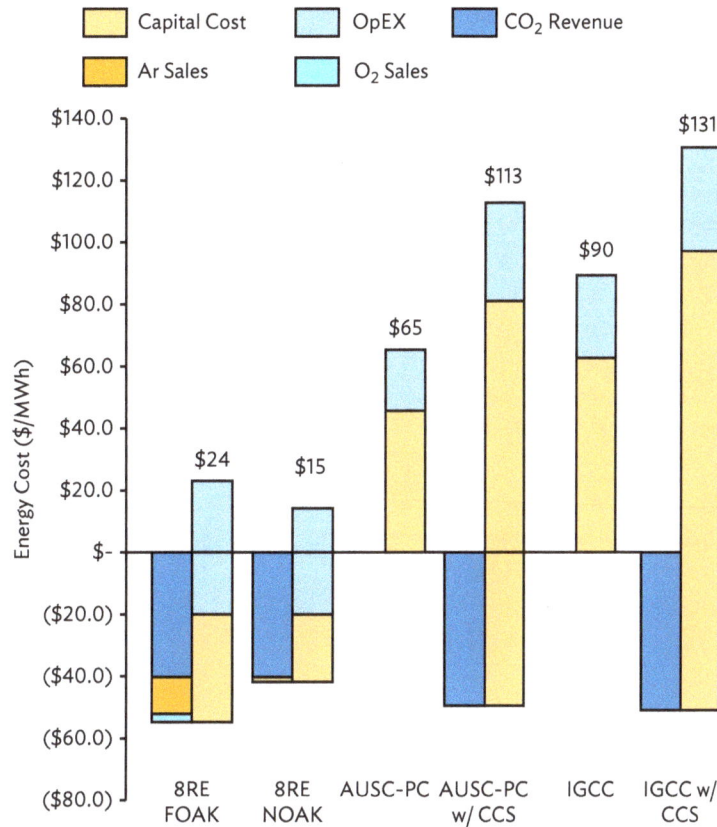

Figure 18:   Allam Cycle Coal Levelized Cost of Power in the United States Market

8RE FOAK = 8 Rivers Energy first of a kind, 8RE NOAK = 8 Rivers Energy new of a kind, Ar = argon, AUSC-PC = advanced ultra-supercritical pulverized coal, AUSC-PC w/CCS = advanced ultra-supercritical pulverized coal with carbon capture and storage, CO_2 = carbon dioxide, IGCC = integrated coal gasification combined cycle, IGCC w/CCS = integrated gasification combined cycle with carbon capture and storage, MWh = megawatt-hour, O_2 = oxygen, OpEx = operating expense.
Source: 8 Rivers and NET Power internal calculations.

Multiple projects are in development. Initial deployments of the Allam Cycle in the US will decrease its capital costs to allow Allam Cycle coal and NET Power to compete with conventional coal and gas plants without relying on strong CO_2 incentives, which makes this technology an important solution for emerging economies which are not able to pay higher costs for electricity. Given the low cost and low pollution profile of the Allam Cycle, it has the potential to become the standard technology for new-build fossil generating power plants going forward, across Asia and globally.

Status and next steps

(i)   The natural gas fired Allam Cycle has been fully demonstrated and is ready for full scale commercialization with multiple 270–300 MW scale plants under development in the US, Europe, and around the world. Commissioning of the first commercial scale NET Power plant is expected in 2024.

(ii)   The coal and biomass-fired Allam Cycle runs on syngas and is expected to undergo a 2-year program to design and test a specific syngas combustor. Early stage project development will continue during this final testing period and commercial scale plants are expected to move toward financial close after the syngas combustor testing is complete.

Challenges in scale-up and deployment

(i) Additional investors could help fund development activities of early projects—including permitting, or detailed engineering—to accelerate the path of these projects to a final investment decision. Additionally, the source of project-level equity and debt will also be key for each of these projects to financially close and begin construction.

(ii) Identification of suitable power plant sites with available fuel supply, CO_2 store, and power offtake infrastructure would also help to expand the number of projects under development.

Technology provider background

8 Rivers created the company NET Power to commercialize the natural gas Allam Cycle and has garnered over $150 million between its four investors: 8 Rivers, Exelon, McDermott, and Oxy Low Carbon Ventures. NET Power built a successful 50 MW thermal plant in La Porte, Texas that achieved combustor first fire in 2018. This technology has the potential to sell power competitively priced to conventional power plants while releasing zero emissions. Today, multiple 270–300 MW scale NET Power plants are in early-stage development around the world.

Contact person: Adam Goff
Principal 8 Rivers Capital
Policy Director at NET Power
Adam.goff@8rivers.com
267-528-8471

Suggestions for further reading

- A. Goff, X. Lu, and J. Fetvedt. 2020. *Pre-FEED Final Report*. https://netl.doe.gov/sites/default/files/2020-06/8-Rivers-Capital-Final-Pre-FEED-Report-Allam-Cycle-Coal-%20 8924331RFE000015-Public-Version-May-19.pdf.
- NET Power. 2020. www.NETPower.com.
- 8 Rivers. 2020. https://8rivers.com/.

Game-Changing Carbon Dioxide Utilization and Storage Technology

CarbonCure Technology

Technology provider
CarbonCure Technologies Inc. (CarbonCure)

Technology description
The proprietary technology of CarbonCure injects recycled carbon dioxide (CO_2) captured from waste emissions by industrial gas suppliers into fresh concrete during production (Figure 19). Once injected the CO_2 converts into a nanomineral in a process known as CO_2 mineralization and becomes permanently trapped. The trapped CO_2 improves the compressive strength of the concrete, allowing for cement reduction while maintaining strength requirements and without impacting performance. Producers could optimize their mix designs and gain competitive advantages while reducing the carbon footprint of concrete structures.

Technology highlights and advantages

(i)   Producers can optimize concrete mix designs.
(ii) Compatible with other green concrete production processes, such as using supplementary cementitious materials.
(iii) CarbonCure concrete reduces CO_2 emissions by approximately 17–20 kilograms (kg) per cubic meter, compared to standard concrete.
(iv) Durable low-carbon concrete allows producers to differentiate and deliver on the sustainability objectives of society.

Potential application in Asia and other regions
The vision of CarbonCure is for post-industrial CO_2-mineralized concrete to become the global standard and to reduce CO_2 emissions by 500+ megatons per year.

Status and next steps

(i) Commercial installations: 300+ concrete producers throughout Canada, the United States, Latin America, and Southeast Asia.
(ii) CarbonCure Concrete Production: 6+ million cubic meters.

Figure 19:   CarbonCure Retrofit Technology

CarbonCure Ready Mix System. CarbonCure technology for concrete production is shown in the foreground (photo by CarbonCure Technologies Inc.).

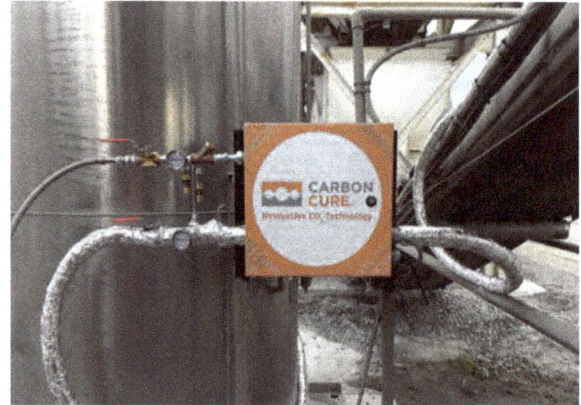

Carbon utilization. CarbonCure technology and carbon dioxide storage tank (photo by CarbonCure Technologies Inc.).

(iii) CO_2 emissions saved: 80+ million kg.
(iv)   Expansion via channel partners to 35 new markets including Australia; the People's Republic of China; Hong Kong, China; Malaysia; Taipei,China; Thailand; and Viet Nam.
(v)   Portfolio of carbon utilization technologies for the concrete manufacturing industry are in varying stages of commercialization.

Challenges in scale-up and deployment
Support in securing regulatory approval is required for scale-up and deployment in new markets.

Related costs

(i)   CarbonCure Technology delivers a rapid return on investment.
(ii)   Producers can reduce cement to offset technology adoption costs.

Technology provider background
Established in 2007, CarbonCure Technologies is a global leader in CO_2 utilization for the concrete industry. Its head office is in Halifax, Nova Scotia, Canada.

Major Achievements of CarbonCure include:

(i)   2020 Cleantech Company of the Year (North America), awarded by the Cleantech Group.
(ii)   Finalist in the NRG COSIA Carbon XPRIZE Competition.
(iii)   A global network of 300+ concrete producer partners.
(iv)   Collectively, over 80+ million kg of CO_2 emissions have been saved as at October 2020.

Contact information:
E-mail: info@carboncure.com

Suggestion for further reading
CarbonCure. 2020. www.carboncure.com.

Game-Changing Carbon Dioxide Capture, Utilization, and Storage Technology Enabler

CCUS KickStarter

Enabler
Oil and Gas Climate Initiative

Description of initiative
Oil and Gas Climate Initiative (OGCI) launched CCUS KickStarter in 2019. KickStarter is an approach—building on the work of many others—that is designed to accelerate collaboration and commercialize CCUS by helping to get multiple low-carbon industrial hubs into operation around the world. As shown in Figure 20, these hubs will capture CO_2 from several industrial sources within one region, sharing transport and storage infrastructure. This approach is not new, but OGCI gained considerable insights into what is needed as it worked on the Clean Gas Project, a forerunner to the Net Zero Teesside hub.

The OGCI KickStarter team is working with governments and across industry sectors to help put in place the necessary market conditions for investments in hubs and projects by member companies, governments, the Climate Investments fund, and other independent investors.

(i)   One group is setting up teams on the ground, building on the work of many others to kickstart high-potential CCUS hubs. The initial aim of OGCI is to get five of these emerging hubs into operation.
(ii)   Another group is building a pipeline of potential future hubs, identifying clusters of emissions sources and sinks in around 25 additional countries. OGCI will focus on maturing some of these by investing in anchor projects and convening others to generate interest. OGCI also aims to help other organizations to collaborate and take the lead in establishing new CCUS hubs.

To this end, learnings will be shared proactively among hubs.

The initial five hubs of KickStarter are the following:

(i)   Net Zero Teesside, United Kingdom
(ii)   Northern Lights, Norway
(iii)   Rotterdam, Netherlands
(iv)   China-Northwest, People's Republic of China
(v)   Gulf of Mexico, United States

Box 11: Oil and Gas Climate Initiative CCUS KickStarter Key Features

Initiative Highlights

- Creates a common CO_2 infrastructure for transportation and storage of CO_2 – results in significant saving of transport infrastructure and fulfills one of the conditions of CCS-readiness
- Potentially enabling a CCUS industry that can store annually 25 times more CO_2 in 2030 than is currently stored today

Sectors of Application

- All industrial emitters

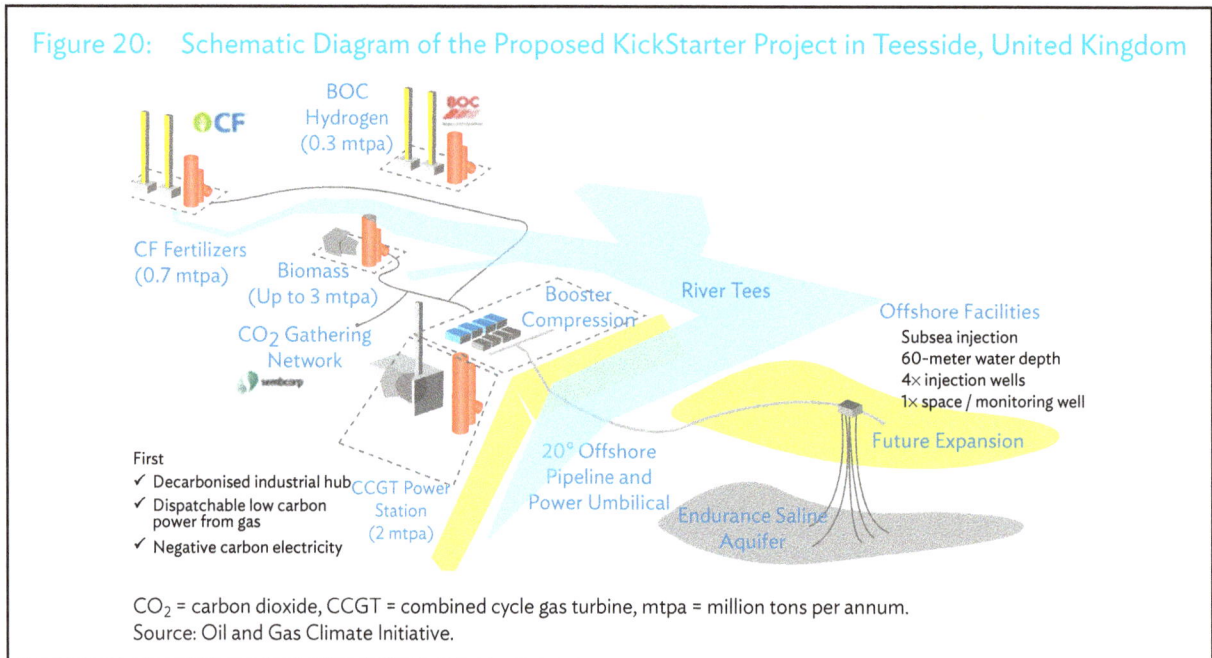

Figure 20:   Schematic Diagram of the Proposed KickStarter Project in Teesside, United Kingdom

CO_2 = carbon dioxide, CCGT = combined cycle gas turbine, mtpa = million tons per annum.
Source: Oil and Gas Climate Initiative.

Advantages and highlights of the initiative

The 20 or so large-scale CCUS facilities in operation today have proved the concept but have not kickstarted a commercial marketplace that would allow a CCUS industry to emerge that can store annually 25 times more carbon dioxide in 2030 than is currently stored today, according to the International Energy Agency. Most of these captured emissions will need to come from hard-to-abate industrial sectors such as cement, steel, and chemicals.

The KickStarter approach focuses its efforts on achieving three conditions for scale-up:

(i)   Economies of scale through shared transport and storage infrastructure.
(ii)   Involvement of government, industry, and nongovernment organizations to build consensus on how to create market conditions that will encourage emitters to capture CO_2 and operators to store it.
(iii)   Commercial credibility by involving large-scale investors who are committed to invest.

Once these hubs are operational, the availability of carbon capture know-how and storage capacity is likely to attract a range of net-zero companies active in clean industry, carbon utilization, and negative emissions (through direct air capture and biomass with CCS).

Potential application in Asia and the world

The KickStarter approach can be used wherever there is an industrial region with substantial carbon dioxide emissions, storage options (onshore, offshore, or by ship), policymakers willing to work on policies and regulations to enable CCUS as a decarbonization tool, and emitters that are aiming to reduce their emissions. Once one hub is in place, it is easier to multiply hubs in that jurisdiction. For OGCI involvement, a member company would need to have some kind of operations in the country, but the approach can be used beyond these companies.

The potential in the People's Republic of China, India, Indonesia, the Republic of Korea, Malaysia, Singapore, Thailand, Viet Nam, and the Gulf Cooperation Council States is significant, with these Asian countries plus Japan active in the Clean Energy Ministerial CCUS Initiative.

Status and next steps

The status of the initial five hubs is given below. OGCI has progressed each of these KickStarter hubs in 2020 and has started work on several new ones.

(i)   **Net Zero Teesside, United Kingdom.** Front end engineering and design is planned for late 2020. The anchor project (abated dispatchable gas power with collective pipelines and offshore storage) is led by bp with Eni, Equinor, Shell, and Total having taken over from OGCI Climate Investments. The government is continuing to develop policies to support the hub. There is interest from emitters in biomass power, fertilizers, petrochemicals, and hydrogen. The hub could potentially store over 10 million tons of CO_2 ($mtCO_2$)/year by 2030.

(ii) **Northern Lights/Longship, Norway.** Final investment decision in 2020. The anchor project (carbon transport by ship and offshore storage) is led by Equinor, Shell, and Total. The project has government support. There is interest from emitters in cement, waste incineration, and beyond. The hub could potentially store 5 $mtCO_2$/year by 2030.

(iii) **Rotterdam, Netherlands.** Investment decisions on the government-supported Porthos anchor project in 2021 are focusing on capture options in refineries and hydrogen production, and on providing storage expertise. The hub could potentially store 10 $mtCO_2$/year by 2030.

(iv) **China-Northwest, People's Republic of China.** A pilot project is being led by CNPC to capture emissions from refineries, chemicals, and power, providing transport and storage infrastructure. The hub could potentially store over 3 $mtCO_2$/year by 2030.

(v)   **Gulf of Mexico, United States.** Working to identify two or more hubs in Louisiana and Texas, in an area that emits over 200 $mtCO_2$/year from refineries, hydrogen, chemicals, power, and fertilizers. Bp, Chevron, ExxonMobil, Occidental, Repsol, Shell, and Total are involved.

Key challenges in scale-up

(i)   **Policies.** Government authorities must be willing to incentivize carbon capture and CO_2 storage as a clean energy solution. This requires a combination of clear reference to CCUS targets in national climate strategies together with policy and regulatory mechanisms such as carbon valuation mechanisms (taxes, trading scheme, performance standard, etc.), subsidies, incentives (tax credits, contract for difference, etc.), and facilities to support international emissions trading linked with CCUS credits. Otherwise, there is little incentive for emitters or operators to act.

(ii) **Regulations.** Many practical issues need to be resolved before a hub can get started. These include storage characterization, reporting requirements, access to pore space, and accepted methodologies for quantifying containment risks.

(iii) **Collaboration.** Close communication is required between diverse stakeholders over many years to move ahead with a hub. That requires local coalitions to bring together emitters, potential investors, and operators while working in the community to build public support and trust.

Enabler background

The Oil and Gas Climate Initiative (OGCI) was launched in 2014. It is a CEO-led consortium that aims to accelerate the industry response to climate change. OGCI member companies explicitly support the Paris Agreement and its goals. As leaders in the industry—accounting for over 30% of global operated oil and gas production—OGCI aims to leverage its collective strength and expand the pace and scope of its transitions to a low-carbon future, so helping to achieve net zero emissions as early as possible.

OGCI members collectively invest over $7 billion each year in low carbon solutions. OGCI Climate Investments—a $1 billion+ fund—invests in solutions to decarbonize sectors like oil and gas, industrials, and commercial transport. OGCI members include bp, Chevron, CNPC, Eni, Equinor, ExxonMobil, Occidental, Petrobras, Repsol, Saudi Aramco, Shell, and Total.

Contact person:
Iain Macdonald
CCUS Workstream Lead
E-mail: Iain.Macdonald2@shell.com

Suggestions for further reading

- Oil and Gas Climate Initiative. 2019. *Scaling Up Action—Aiming for net zero emissions.* https:// oilandgasclimateinitiative.com/wp-content/ uploads/2019/10/OGCI-Annual-Report-2019.pdf.
- IEA Environmental Projects Ltd. (IEAGHG). 2013. *CO_2 Pipeline Infrastructure.* https://ieaghg.org/docs/ General_Docs/Reports/2013-18.pdf.
- Oil and Gas Climate Initiative. 2020. *Action and Engagement. Removing carbon dioxide.* https:// oilandgasclimateinitiative.com/action-and-engagement/ccus/.
- Earth Resources. 2020. *The CarbonNet Project.* https://earthresources.vic.gov.au/projects/ carbonnet-project.